MW00716094

The Man with the
White Beard

© 2014, Bruce Templeton

 Canada Council Conseil des Arts
for the Arts du Canada

Canadä

Newfoundland
Labrador

We gratefully acknowledge the financial support of the Canada Council for the Arts,
the Government of Canada through the Canada Book Fund (CBF),
and the Government of Newfoundland and Labrador through the Department
of Tourism, Culture and Recreation for our publishing program.

Cover Design by Todd Manning • Layout by Joanne Snook-Hann
Printed on acid-free paper

Published by
CREATIVE PUBLISHERS
an imprint of CREATIVE BOOK PUBLISHING
a Transcontinental Inc. associated company
P.O. Box 8660, Stn. A
St. John's, Newfoundland and Labrador A1B 3T7

Printed in Canada by: Marquis imprimeur inc.

Library and Archives Canada Cataloguing in Publication

Templeton, Bruce, author
    The man with the white beard / Bruce Templeton.

Sequel to: The man in the red suit.
ISBN 978-1-77103-053-3 (bound)

    1. Christmas. 2. Children--Hospitals--Newfoundland and
Labrador--St. John's. 3. Rotary International. 4. Poliomyelitis--
Vaccination. 5. Templeton, Bruce. 6. St. John's (N.L.)--Biography.
I. Title.

GT4985.T443 2014   394.2663   C2014-904692-8

A Memoir

The Man with the
White Beard

BRUCE TEMPLETON

Foreword by Sister Elizabeth M. Davis, RSM

St. John's, Newfoundland and Labrador, 2014

It is one thing to understand the spirit of Christmas, but it is another to live and share it all year round. The Man With the White Beard *takes the reader on Templeton's never-ending journey to bring love, caring and joy to children and families in Newfoundland and Labrador and beyond. Join Bruce Templeton for a rare trip on board Santa's sleigh, exploring the true meaning of the season as only Templeton can show us.*

Toni-Marie Wiseman
NTV News

Sometimes life's journey takes us to many different places with our most precious relationships. For me, Christmas has always been a time of renewal for those relationships. Bruce's first book, and now again with this second book, are well-crafted tales that will bring you back to the relationships we cherish – the love of family and friends – through the magic of Santa Claus. Stories of wonderful moments are told, reminding us all of the power of love and kindness.

Cathy Bennett, MHA

This is a book to touch the heart. The real life experiences of The Man With the White Beard, our own special Santa, Bruce Templeton, are often poignant, sometimes amusing and always inspiring. They will bring home to the reader the real meaning and magic of Christmas – love, generosity and being truly present for others. I have seen this amazing man in action. If this book does not put you in touch with your inner child and make you think about the way we celebrate Christmas, nothing will. A book to be shared!

Shannie Duff
Former Deputy Mayor of St. John's, NL

I dedicate this book to Rotary International and its Polio Plus program. Join us in the world effort to "End Polio Now." Let's support the many dedicated volunteers who are working to eradicate this crippling disease. There are only three countries left and we are "this close" to a victory.

Table of Contents

SANTA CLAUS OATH:
I pledge myself to these principles as a
descendant of St. Nicholas, the gift-giver of Myra.

SANTA CLAUS OATH:
I know the "real reason for the season" and know
that I am blessed to be able to be a part of it.

SANTA CLAUS OATH:
I promise to use "my" powers to create happiness, spread
love and make fantasies come to life in the true and
sincere tradition of the Santa Claus Legend.

SANTA CLAUS OATH:
I will seek knowledge to be well versed in the mysteries
of bringing Christmas cheer and goodwill to all
the people that I encounter in my journeys and travels.

Foreword

Seventeen hundred years ago in Asia Minor, Nicholas, the Bishop of Myra, showed extraordinary kindness and generosity to those in need. In the Middle Ages in Holland, on the Eve of the Feast of St. Nicholas, the bishop (in Dutch "Sinterklaas") would come from heaven and visit children in their homes, giving gifts to those who had been good. Four hundred years ago in England, Father Christmas, a kindly old gentleman, invited adults to celebrate, was hospitable and generous to poor people and wore a furred gown and cap. Two hundred years ago in France, on Christmas Eve, children left their shoes by the fireplace filled with carrots for Père Noël's donkey, knowing that Père Noël would take the treats and leave presents instead. Two hundred years ago in the United States, Santa Claus appeared as a portly, joyous, white-bearded man wearing a red coat, white-cuffed trousers and black boots, riding from the North Pole on Christmas Eve in a sleigh pulled by reindeer and carrying a bag full of gifts for children. Surely these legends were only meant to entertain children. Bruce Templeton's *The Man with the White Beard* proves otherwise.

Stories, images and traditions are not only a means of celebrating joy and hope, they also shape who we are as people, families, corporations and communities. This book, the sequel to *The Man in the Red Suit*, is evidence of the ability of one person to make a difference. It reminds us of the goodness in our world, and invites all of us to help make it a better place. Through Bruce's narration, and through the voices of children and adults who he meets on his shared journey with Santa, we come to see the evidence, and accept that invitation.

These stories are not sentimental, simplistic or Pollyanna-like. They bring us into the world of real people to whom we are introduced by name – a child with cancer, an infant who dies, a child who loses a beloved pet, an adult with an addiction, and a family of ten with few financial resources. These same stories introduce us to those who care – the nurses and physicians at the children's hospital, the inmates at the penitentiary who build the Christmas floats, the airline that provides transportation for children to visit Santa at the North Pole, and the radio station that supports that visit. We meet the hotel where free rooms are provided for a distraught family, the corporations that donate money and the staff members who donate their time. And we enjoy the candy-stripers who teach Santa to dance, a translator who helps him speak to a French child, and the numerous children who ask many challenging and interesting questions.

The connection between the suffering and the caring is Santa – the person, the symbol, and the image. He is the one who creates happiness and spreads love, who learns where the need is greatest, the one who travels 900 kilometres to visit the grave of a child, and the one who calls forth the best in all of us.

The connection between Santa and the reader is made through the stories in this book.

Through the act of reading, a person and a community can discover, define and re-define itself. Bruce Templeton's story is not a simple one. In the thirty-six years since this Santa journey began, he has visited children's hospitals more than fifteen hundred times. He is donating the proceeds from the sales of the first printing to Rotary International in its efforts to eradicate polio in the last three countries where it remains an epidemic. He uses the beautiful Santa Claus Oath to frame his gathering of stories, and he challenges us to make our own pledge to "create happiness, spread love and make fantasies come to life." By his words, but even more by his example, he is inviting us to find our own way of embracing the Santa journey, and of making a difference in the lives of people we meet every day.

Who could have ever imagined that a bishop would be remembered after fourteen hundred years and not for his teaching or his miracles, but for his everyday acts of kindness? Who could have ever anticipated that this memory would be captured in the image of an elderly man in a colourful costume, arriving just once a year and giving gifts with no expectation of anything in return? Who could ever have imagined that this simple annual visit would come to symbolize goodness, service, precious memories, unconditional love and hope for peace? In *The Man with the White Beard*, Bruce Templeton has captured the memory, the joy and the hope created by this symbol through the voices and stories of real people. Together with the children and the adults whose voices echo throughout the pages of this book, we say humbly, "Thank you, Santa."

Sister Elizabeth M. Davis, RSM

Preface

The book you hold in your hands is a sequel to the memoir I wrote several years ago, *The Man in the Red Suit.* The impact of the first book was very gratifying. In fact, many readers contacted me and asked about the children they met within its pages. Where are they now? Am I still in touch with these families? I had to think carefully about the best way to answer those letters and emails. There were also details about Santa's visits during recent years that created special moments. Some of these stories are happy and some are sad, but all of them needed to be told. The result is *The Man with the White Beard.*

I am grateful to everyone who has written, emailed, or called, and especially those who have shared their experience of being in a particular hospital on Christmas Eve when Santa came to visit. Although I use the word "ministry" very cautiously, I feel that my work during the holiday season – attending to children and their families at Christmas – is a form of service. This is a privilege and a responsibility I do not take lightly.

I am more convinced than ever about the message I offered in my first book: *It is your presence – and not presents – that really counts at Christmas.* Everyone celebrates this special day in a unique way. This is never more true than when a young family member is in the hospital. Sometimes the families of these children come to my book signings to share memories of their special hospital visit from Santa. These are the "then and now" stories, where I am frequently shown a photo with Santa from twenty or thirty years ago in the neo-natal or intensive care unit. The person standing in front of me often says, "And look at me now, Santa!"

The Man in the Red Suit seemed to have a powerful impact on some readers. Here is just one of those examples. A very successful business owner (and personal friend) had planned a short vacation with her family in Florida. The idea was to see Disney World in two days. Together they figured it could be done if they got an early start each morning and walked until dusk. Earlier, my friend had purchased a copy of *The Man in the Red Suit* and read it on the plane from St. John's to Orlando, Florida. She smiled and cried for half the flight.

Late on the second day of the Disney World tour, my friend's exhausted kids looked at her and said, "Mom, we haven't seen half of it yet." She thought about her children and what she had read. "*It is your presence – and not presents – that counts.*" My friend turned to her partner and said, "I can stay if you can." Then she called her office to tell them she would not be able to attend the December board meetings booked for the following week. She turned off her cellphone – and they all jumped on the nearest roller-coaster, laughing and giggling all the way.

This kind of change in attitude is encouraging. But there is another – and equally important – reason for creating this new book. The author royalties from the first printing of *The Man in the Red Suit* were donated to a cause close to my heart. Vaccine for more than 200,000 children has been purchased to immunize against polio in Pakistan, Afghanistan and Nigeria. This was achieved through the donation of those funds, the efforts of other Rotary Clubs, the support of Rotary International, and the World Health Organization. Through the magic of matching donations, Rotary International has been able to continue its great work in the "End Polio Now" campaign. From every book sale from the first printing, three children somewhere in the world are now safe from polio. With some additional proceeds from this sequel, I hope we can continue to do that good work.

Many readers may be too young to remember the disfiguring disease Poliomyelitis – commonly called polio – but their parents or grandparents will certainly know about it. Rotary International took an early interest in funding research to eliminate this crippling disease. In the 1950s, Rotary members heard encouraging news from Dr. Jonas Salk at the University of Pittsburgh about his research. Four years later, a vaccine was approved for mass use in the United States. But it was not until the 1988 annual meeting of the World Health Assembly that a

Dr. Bruce Aylward (right) Assistant Director-General, Polio and Emergencies at the World Health Organization, chats with the author.

motion was passed to launch a global polio eradication initiative. At the time, polio was endemic in 125 countries. The initiative called for the eradication of the disease by the year 2000. (Fortunately, Rotary International had already been doing this work for a decade.) In 1979, Rotary clubs took on a project to buy and help deliver polio vaccine to more than 6 million children in the Philippines.

In 1997, the last case of polio occurred in the Western Pacific Region in a fifteen-month-old girl named Mum Chanty who lived near Phnom Penh, Cambodia. In 2000, a record 550 million children – almost one-tenth of the world's population – had received the oral polio vaccine. In 2003, six countries remained polio-endemic: Afghanistan, Egypt, India, Niger, Nigeria and Pakistan. Three years later, in 2006, the number of polio-endemic countries dropped to four (Pakistan, Afghanistan, India, Nigeria), the lowest levels in human history. Then, in 2012, India recorded an entire year without a recorded case of polio and was finally taken off the polio endemic list.

Medical practitioners now say we are "this close" to eradicating the disease. However, for the three countries where the battle is not won, there will be no easy victories. The dedication of the immunization teams is absolutely astonishing. There are big risks, and volunteers have died in their efforts to bring vaccine to children. Sometimes, with weapons pointed at them, the volunteers have been told to take the vaccine first before it is given to the children. Yet these brave souls continue to do their work.

When *The Man in the Red Suit* was published in 2012, my wife Paula and I made a decision to use the proceeds of sales from the first printing for Rotary's "End Polio Now" Campaign. In 2013, additional funds were donated from a related activity.

Santa does many visits each year, and some of them are to corporate offices. There is never a fee for the visits, but I am often asked the same question: "And how will we pay you, Santa?" The simple response is to make a donation to Rotary International's Polio Plus Campaign.

Rotarian Stella Roy administering polio vaccine in Nigeria.

The Bill and Melinda Gates Foundation has been (and continues to be) at Rotary's side in the drive to eliminate polio. Their foundation has been generously matching (or exceeding) the dollars raised by Rotary International. Other institutions (including the local Rotary Clubs) match as well. Often one dollar raised by a Rotary organization can quickly become three because of the matching contributions.

So the $40,000 raised locally over two years by my first little book became $120,000 in total donations. With the cost of a vaccine averaging about sixty cents per child, approximately 200,000 children around the world have already been helped. We will continue this work. Thanks to you, my readers, today children somewhere in Nigeria, Afghanistan or Pakistan may receive two drops of vaccine on their tongues. This simple act will change their lives.

Introduction

Although I have been "assisting" Santa Claus for more than three decades, I only recently found out that there is an official "Santa Claus Oath." Those of us who are its signatories are committed to following this code with diligence and respect. The eight principles that make up the Santa Claus Oath reflect the ideals of what assisting Santa should be all about.

The Oath was written and dedicated in 2008 by Phillip L. Wenz, a man commonly referred to as "the child who grew up to be Santa Claus." It reflects the values of two amazing Santas who are role models for us all: Charles W. Howard of New York and Raymond "Jim" Yellig of Santa Claus, Indiana. The Oath has been adopted by nearly every serious Santa Claus organization and by those of us who assist him around the world. By following its principles, we try to "create happiness, spread love and make fantasies come to life in the true and sincere tradition of the Santa Claus Legend."

Here is the Santa Claus Oath, reprinted with special permission.

The Santa Claus Oath

I will seek knowledge to be well versed in the mysteries of bringing Christmas cheer and goodwill to all the people that I encounter in my journeys and travels.

I shall be dedicated to hearing the secret dreams of both children and adults.

I understand that the true and only gift I can give, as Santa, is myself.

I acknowledge that some of the requests I will hear will be difficult and sad. I know in these difficulties there lies an opportunity to bring a spirit of warmth, understanding and compassion.

I know the "real reason for the season" and know that I am blessed to be able to be a part of it.

I realize that I belong to a brotherhood and will be supportive, honest and show fellowship to my peers.

I promise to use "my" powers to create happiness, spread love and make fantasies come to life in the true and sincere tradition of the Santa Claus Legend.

I pledge myself to these principles as a descendant of St. Nicholas, the gift-giver of Myra.
Phillip L. Wenz

In the chapters that follow, I have (with permission) framed each section around one of these oaths. The order of the oaths has been altered in order to convey the arc of my narrative.

In creating a historically accurate symbol for the Oath, one of our goals in developing the Coat of Arms was that it needed to represent the eight principles that make up the Santa Claus Oath.

The eight elements of the Santa Claus Oath Coat of Arms are the Shield, SC Letters, Crossed Candy Canes, Traditional Symbols of Saint Nicholas, Reindeer, Grapevines, Banner and the Colors.

Each element represents the following:

Shield - The shield shape is consistent with the time of Saint Nicholas.

Symbols - The letters S and C represent the name of Santa Claus. The candy canes symbolize the two legendary Santas, Charles Howard and Jim Yellig.

The canes are crossed as Yellig's and Howard's paths crossed only once. The lower part of the shield has the three acknowledged symbols of Saint Nicholas, the miter (bishop's hat) the crosier (shepherds staff) and three gold coins, representing the gold given to provide dowries to impoverished maidens.

Reindeer - There are two reindeer that flank the shield. One reindeer represents designer bearded Santas and the other represents real bearded Santas.
The reindeer have come together in unity to uphold the shield and uphold their pledge to the Santa Claus Oath.

Grapevines - At the top and bottom of the shield and reindeer there are grapevines. The grapevines are an ancient symbol for the thirst and quest of knowledge.

Banner - Completing the Coat of Arms is a banner with "Santa Claus Oath" on it.

Colors - The colors of the Santa Claus Coat of Arms are the traditional Christian colors of Christmas. Red is for the blood of Christ, green is for the eternal life in Christ and gold is for Christ the Divine.

With Permission of Philip L. Wenz

SANTA CLAUS OATH:
I pledge myself to these principles as a
descendant of St. Nicholas, the gift-giver of Myra.

Chapter 1
What should I do now, St. Nicholas?

The display screen on a phone is a pretty helpful invention for most of us. In my case, it gives me a moment to get myself into the right frame of mind for the caller who waits on the line. But there must be business leaders in Newfoundland and Labrador who glance at their display and debate whether to answer the phone when they see the name "Bruce Templeton" on the screen! If it's anytime in the fall season, it means I am up to my eyeballs in Christmas planning and am likely to need their help. Frequently my friends and "elves" are able to offer a solution to my problem. If not, they can often tell me where to find it. (Or they can just tell me where to go – but happily they would never say that to Santa!) Of course, some requests are more difficult to fulfill than others.

Many readers of my first book will know the story of "The Flight to the North Pole," an amazing event that allows eighteen randomly selected children between the ages of five and eight, together with one adult, to go to the North Pole. On a Saturday close to Christmas, the group is taken to St. John's International

Airport to board a plane owned by Provincial Airlines. Once the airplane door is closed, it taxis to the end of the long runway before lifting off into the cold dawn morning, flying off to meet Santa. When they land at the North Pole (or as close as we can get), Santa boards the plane and talks to each one of the children.

Some readers will also remember the amazing people at Steele Communications' Hits 99.1 FM Radio Station. They are the dream-makers who make this event possible. Over the course of the weeks leading up to the trip, a phone call is made to each child who has been selected to be on the plane. The phone calls are broadcast live on the air at roughly 7:45 a.m. As the reserved seats on the plane fill, the tension and excitement in the listening audience mounts. Every one of these children has been lucky enough to have their name picked in a random draw. But there's one exception.

Each year, Santa has a small part to play in the selection of one additional child. The criteria are always the same. It must be a child who is seriously ill, has an inoperable condition, and for whom this may be their last Christmas. Although Santa is allowed to set these guidelines, the selection is actually made with the help of the wonderful professionals at the Janeway Children's Health and Rehabilitation Centre. As with all the children on this special flight, I am not aware of their surnames, and I don't know the medical details of the child chosen from the Janeway. I just know they deserve this special privilege.

In the fall of 2013, I knew that the special guest flying with us to the North Pole was a young girl from the west coast of Newfoundland. She had an inoperable brain tumour. The family was planning to drive 850 kilometres so their child could have a radiation treatment at the hospital on Friday and then join our flight on Saturday morning. Because the child and her family were required to be in St. John's for treatment, the provincial government was committed to giving them financial assistance for their travel costs and accommodations. Everything was set, or so we thought.

On the Tuesday prior to the big day, I got a call from my elf in the Janeway Children's Health and Rehabilitation Centre. She had bad news. Due to unexpected equipment problems, radiation treatments could not be offered that week. The family had been called, and the girl's appointment had been cancelled and rescheduled for a later date. The response from the child's mother was very gracious. She said that Santa should select another child for the flight to the North Pole. They could not afford the cost of the gas or the hotel bill in St. John's without a treatment appointment, and without the financial assistance for which they would normally qualify.

"Our daughter will be heartbroken," she told the hospital, "but she simply can't be on the plane to meet Santa." My elf at the Janeway relayed the conversation with the mother of this child, and ended with a simple question.

"What can you do, St. Nicholas?"

This is the perfect moment for us to think back 1,700 years, to the time of St. Nicholas and to imagine how different he might have been from the character we now know as Santa – who is really only in his eighties. In the famous Washington Irving book *'Twas the Night Before Christmas,* Santa Claus is not mentioned once. St. Nicholas, however, is the patron saint of children, and his stories are legendary. Nicholas, the famous Bishop of Myra, cared so much for children that he gave away almost everything he had.

In 2013, we had to imagine how St. Nicholas might have handled this situation. Fortunately, it helps if you have a good network of friends. Rotary International has an astonishing network of caring people in every profession and every field.

Luckily, Santa's helper in St. John's knows a few Rotarians in the hotel business. The motto for Rotarians is "Service Above Self." Surely one of these hoteliers could offer some help to this family in need.

The first call went out to a Rotary elf who works at the Sheraton Hotel Newfoundland. When she looked at the display screen on her phone, she knew who was calling and she could be pretty sure there would be an "ask" from this modern-day St. Nicholas. She didn't hesitate to take the call. The response from this wonderful helper was immediate and generous. St. Nicholas connected the hotel with the folks at Eastern Health. Then the happy message went back to the family on the west coast of Newfoundland.

"Please get in your car on Friday and drive across the province. The Sheraton Hotel Newfoundland will provide a suite for you and your daughter for the weekend. Your meal costs will be covered as well as your gas bill. Your daughter will still be on the flight to meet Santa."

These are the gifts of St. Nicholas – but they are really gifts from good people all around us. They are a demonstration of the generosity offered by a business community that has never failed to support St. Nicholas' efforts. It has little to do with buying gifts and everything to do with keeping dreams alive. It is when someone responds to a call for help and displays great kindness that the St. Nicholas spirit is alive and well.

Chapter 2
Can Santa help a large family?

After so many years of assisting Santa, I've seen that certain informal traditions have started to take root at Christmastime. Many people and corporations call my office asking me to direct where they should donate money and presents. It is left for me to decide what to do with these lovely gifts. Even when I ask if they have a favourite charity, these kind souls offer the same reply. "Santa, you know where the need is the greatest."

Sometimes, it can be hard to find those in real need. Yes, there are families who register at food banks and who receive support through traditional avenues. However, some people choose not to use the help of these agencies. And, that's when Santa gets interesting phone calls and the chance to match the gifts from the anonymous donors to the families who need the support, but don't always look for it.

I clearly recall one such example. I got an email from a church group who told me there was a large family that could use a helping hand. A member of the congregation had gone to their minister to make him aware of this family's plight – even though they were not members of the congregation. In fact, the family was clearly not looking for support; the last thing they said they wanted was charity. Still, it was hard for anyone who knew them not to see the obvious need.

First, there was the sheer size of the family: ten children, with five girls between the ages of five and thirteen, and five boys between the ages of eight and eighteen. There was also an enormous health challenge to overcome. The children's mother had breast cancer and was undergoing chemo and radiation treatments. Despite her condition, the mother was doing her very best for the children. She drove them to school, and they came home for lunch each day because the family could not afford even a modestly-priced school lunch program.

The school was doing what it could to help and had purchased bicycles for the children. The community was doing its part, too. The local dentist offered to look after their dental needs. Several times a year he also quietly delivered four or five large pizzas to their house. In the winter, the family kept their poorly-insulated house only as warm as they could afford, so the children would often wear multiple sweaters. They seemed almost oblivious to their situation.

The children spent a lot of time playing outside in the yard with their little dog. The boys also liked to skate, and play hockey and soccer. The church office said the family had never so much as asked for a loaf of bread. They did their best to survive. The father had a low-paying, steady job. But he did not drive, which was a real challenge with ten active children.

A social worker was asked by the church to let them know the family's greatest need. The response was, "Today, it is toilet paper." The older kids were working and contributing what they could, but there was still not enough income. They just needed a helping hand, "a leg up," as the saying goes. Meanwhile, help was being mustered not far away.

For many years, Santa has received a call from a very large metal refining company. The message is – happily – always the same. Each year more than 200 employees bring presents into a very large office and place them under the Christmas tree.

"Santa, you must know where there is the greatest need," they say to me. "Where should we deliver the toys?"

The magic of Christmas starts to unfold as the toys are first delivered to a neutral location, where they are organized by age and gender. I made a call to the church mentioned above, and a representative picked up a donation of items that were suitable for this large family. The rest of the gifts went to a Toy Lending Library (which is a great way to share with *lots* of children).

As readers are now well aware, Santa leans heavily on his friends at the Rotary Club of St. John's. Every year this wonderful group organizes a Christmas Hamper project. The work starts in October when the club is told how many hampers will be needed by December. In this particular year it was 350. At a cost of eighty dollars per hamper, the fundraising needs to start early and the money is carefully spent. Eventually, a great team comes together for an amazing twenty-four-hour work-a-thon from noon on a Friday through to noon on Saturday.

All Friday afternoon, boxes donated by a local manufacturer are carefully assembled. Three hundred and fifty tops and bottoms have to be folded and taped, which is a lot of work! Next, the non-perishable items are delivered to the hall by wholesalers who offer exceptional value within our $28,000 budget. Potatoes, carrots, turnip, peas, salt meat, cabbage and apple pies are lined up on long trestle tables. Outside, at the hall's entrance, the reception area is made ready. Due to the privacy act, we do not know the names of our hamper recipients. We only know that by noon on Saturday, 350 families will come to the hall either by car or on foot to receive a box of food which can weigh up to fifty pounds. The food hampers are designed for families of all sizes. None of the recipients will have to go without a Christmas meal. The families are selected by the provincial government's income support division, and they have a slip of paper which only tells us the size of the hamper.

There is, of course, one more key component to this project. At 7 a.m. on Saturday morning, just before the hall opens, trucks arrive with a mountain of frozen turkeys. When the doors open at 8 a.m., those in line receive their Christmas hamper and a turkey, while generous Rotarians make themselves available to assist anyone who would like a drive home with their heavy load.

One year, a lady took a hamper box but struggled to get it to the front door. Outside, she opened a large knapsack and started putting the food from the box into the pack. A Rotarian came along to ask if he could help. She explained that she lived seven kilometres up a hill near St. John's in the community of Shea Heights. She said the family had no money for gas, so she had borrowed her son's bicycle to ride down the hill to pick up the hamper. Now she was going to pedal back home up that same hill.

My fellow Rotarian asked if he could put her bicycle in his truck and drive her home. A female Rotarian was found to accompany them, as is the required protocol. Safely at home at the top of the hill, and with the hamper in her small kitchen, she turned to them both and said, "Thank you, blessed angels. You have just made Christmas for my family."

My friend said she was reminded of an old saying: *There but for the grace of God go I.*

Chapter 3
Santa, can you do magic?

Sometimes children ask Santa really challenging questions, and these require a lot of thought. You want to answer truthfully, but you don't want to spoil the wonderful sense of mystery that surrounds Christmas. You certainly cannot lie, nor can Santa ever give an assurance that something will *definitely* happen. So, what do you do when a forlorn little girl asks, "Will you bring my puppy back to life?" Or when a young boy asks, "Will you bring me a baby brother next year so I'll have a friend to play soccer with?"

In these challenging situations, I look for guidance. I try to go back in time and think about St. Nicholas, who was born in 280 AD. That makes him about 1,734 years old! The Santa Claus we see today did not "exist" until roughly 1931, and that makes him only eighty-three. However, the difference between them goes considerably beyond simple age.

The history of St. Nicholas is the story of a young man, orphaned at age seven, who became a priest in his teens, and then Bishop of Myra in his early twenties. His whole life was devoted

to sharing and giving. We have seen many pictures of Nicholas doing good deeds and have heard many legends to describe his works. A number of churches, cathedrals and basilicas have stained glass windows that show St. Nicholas holding a tray with three items on it. Some link that number to the Trinity. Others link it to stories relating to his stature as the patron saint of seafarers and of children.

He is credited with bringing back to life three young boys who were killed by a wicked innkeeper and placed in a barrel of brine. (Not all the stories in the Nicholas history are suitable to be read to children!) Legends also tell of his generosity. In one instance he supported three young women whose father could not provide them with a dowry before marriage, and they faced an uncertain future. But in all of the stories, Nicholas did miraculous work.

So how do we translate the best of the Nicholas tradition into a more modern time? Where is the line between illusion, magic and miracle? How should Santa think, act and behave? Clearly, Santa will go to *almost* any length to keep holiday dreams alive for children. Admittedly, that may involve some degree of illusion, while it probably also requires the support of parents. Here is one of those instances.

When I'm assisting Santa in a classroom full of children, I am occasionally confronted by a pesky child, one who may ask a tough question in front of his friends.

"What is my name, Santa, and what do I really want for Christmas?

I don't apologize for it, but I often have a teacher just outside the classroom door with a radio transmitter. Through my earphones I can hear a response.

"His name is Joshua, and he really hopes his dad will be home off the oil rigs for Christmas."

Joshua is really astonished when Santa looks into his eyes and relays this answer. "Well, Joshua, Santa will do his best and we will see what we can do about getting your dad home for Christmas."

The sponsored flight to the North Pole is also an illusion, but I do wonder what it must be like to be a six-year-old child, flying away on a great adventure. What is it like when the plane touches down and the pilot says he can see Santa outside? And when Santa gets onto the plane, all covered in snow, and walks down the aisle naming every child in every seat and answering their questions about Christmas, is the reaction magical, or is it miraculous because of the communal kindness that makes the moment possible?

There is definitely illusion involved in the Santa Claus Parade when my chief elf, Paula, walks ahead of the float as she has done for thirty-five years. Carefully, she chooses a child and a parent from the 60,000 people at the parade and quietly approaches the parent. Then moments later, I hear through my earphones, "Santa, on your right, on her father's shoulders, the child in the purple snowsuit is Amanda. She is four years old." Santa turns to the right. From fourteen feet off the pavement he looks down and says, "Merry Christmas, Amanda. You look warm in your purple snowsuit."

Yes, the illusion can be explained, but what about the magic? Why do wonderful businesses donate milk and cookies to a whole school of elementary students in response to one child asking her mother why they can't afford to put out treats for Santa on Christmas Eve? Why do the people who now come to the Santa Claus Parade each year bring more than ten tons of groceries to stock the Community Food Sharing services in Newfoundland and Labrador? And what about the honest-to-goodness miracles?

I was sitting in a busy traffic aisle of a Costco warehouse in October, signing copies of *The Man in the Red Suit*, when a mother and her teenage daughter came along.

"Hi, Santa. Here is a picture of my daughter taken seventeen years ago in the Pediatric Intensive Care Unit on Christmas Eve. She weighed less than 600 grams, and we were told her chances of survival were not good. You held her for her first photo and you saw me clutch the cross I was wearing around my neck. I asked you to pray for her and you said that we should all ask St. Nicholas to be there. 'Don't forget,' you said, 'he is the patron saint of children.' I left my baby in the hospital, and I cried all the way home. I got on my knees and asked St. Nicholas for his help."

Then, with a big smile on her face, this same woman made a simple request.

"Santa, would you sign one of your books for my daughter? Look at her today!"

When I looked up, a beautiful young lady stood on the other side of the table. "Would you sign a book for me, Mr. Templeton? I have heard the stories of my first Christmas all of my life and now I get to meet the first man who ever held me."

Illusions can be explained, but there is true magic when a totally unexpected gesture brings a result beyond all expectations. During more than thirty years of assisting Santa, and through more than 1,500 visits, there have been happy outcomes – many of them involving children and many of those especially on Christmas Eve – where I cannot explain the miracle of how a child survives.

I do believe that St. Nicholas is present at Christmas. His presence is part of the divine mystery that gives us the presents that are *truly* priceless.

SANTA CLAUS OATH:
I know the "real reason for the season" and know
that I am blessed to be able to be a part of it.

Chapter 4
Which one are you, Santa?

This question was asked by a little boy during a party in a church basement a few weeks before Christmas. Santa was standing beside a stained glass window that celebrated the life of St. Nicholas. The minister had just finished explaining to the children who this saint was, and why he was important. The child looked at the depiction of St. Nicholas in the window. Then he looked back at me.

"I'm not sure if I get it," he said.

Frankly, he's not alone. Understanding the differences between St. Nicholas and the more modern Santa Claus can be a challenging task. In *The Man in the Red Suit*, we learned a lot about the life of St. Nicholas and how his life story morphed into the figure we now know as Santa Claus roughly eighty years ago. The Nicholas story goes back many centuries to when he was born in Turkey in the year 280 AD. Both of his parents died when he was just nine years old, and he entered the priesthood and was made a bishop at a very early age. According to his biographers, he received an inheritance, but he was troubled about his new wealth.

"How can I stop feeling guilty about having so many things when my neighbours have nothing?" he is said to have asked a friend. Judging by the answer, it seems his friend was a wise man.

"Go quietly. Listen and learn what the community needs, and satisfy that need where you can. Do it with love, grace and humility, and do it anonymously. Serve with no expectation of anything in return."

St. Nicholas took this good advice and lived according to these principles. When he died on December 6, 343 AD, at the age of sixty-three, he was mourned by all those whose lives he had touched. Soon, the story of his good works and generosity spread. The spirit of St. Nicholas had been released into the world.

But it is a long journey from Bishop Nicholas to Santa flying in a sleigh with reindeer. Fortunately, there are other stories that help us understand the modern traditions about Christmas stockings, St. Nicholas in the "New World," and the many ways in which we describe this jolly old fellow and his gift-giving. For example, three years before he died, St. Nicholas came upon a cottage where there was smoke coming out of the chimney. When he knocked and entered, Nicholas found socks drying in front of the fire. On a whim, he decided to leave toys for the children in the socks. That was probably the origin of "the stockings were hung by the chimney with care..."

On August 3, 1492, Queen Isabella funded Christopher Columbus to set sail with three ships to explore for new lands.

St. Nicholas is the patron saint of seafarers, and Columbus no doubt invoked his spirit to accompany them on his voyage. In 1497, John Cabot landed at Bonavista, Newfoundland. It's comforting to think that the spirit of Nicholas was somehow on board the ship when it arrived in this part of the world.

Thirty years later, King Henry VIII got into a battle with the church when it would not allow his divorce from Catherine. So, the King established the Church of England and married Anne Boleyn. Saints such as Nicholas were not welcome in this new church. Parents and religious leaders had to come up with new explanations for the way children received their gifts. New terms such as "Father Christmas" and "Père Noel" were thus created.

In 1621, the main Dutch settlement in North America was at Fort Orange, in what is now the State of New York. It was the Dutch, learning to speak English, who have been credited with creating the words "Santa Claus" from "Sinterklaas." The name Santa Claus itself came from the Dutch *Sinterklaas*, a variation of *Sinter Niklaas* meaning St. Nicholas. When Dutch immigrants came to the United States, they brought their holiday traditions with them, including the tradition of Sinterklaas, and of giving gifts on December 6th, Saint Nicholas Day.

The name Kris Kringle came from the German *Christkindl* or *Christkindlein*, which means "Christ Child." It was Martin Luther who became concerned that St. Nicholas was starting to overshadow Jesus Christ and so the Christ Child was introduced.

What about the carol traditions at Christmas? What is their origin? In Germany, at a mass in St. Nicholas Church in Oberndorf held on December 25, 1818, two men named Franz Gruber and Father Mohr stood before their congregation. Father Mohr held a sheet of paper and sang tenor. Franz Gruber played the guitar and sang bass. For the first time, the words and melody of *Silent Night, Holy Night* were introduced to the world.

There is also the famous children's book associated with Christmas. In 1822, Clement Moore's daughter, Charity, asked her father to write her a poem. As he considered the task, he looked out the window and saw the family gardener. Jan Duyckinck, the man weeding the garden, was a Dutch descendent. He had a white beard and was a little overweight, but he did his work cheerfully as he smoked on a little pipe. Duyckinck is thought to be the character that Moore describes in his famous poem. This lovely piece of verse for Charity was called "A Visit from St. Nicholas." As most of us know, it begins: "'Twas the night before Christmas and all through the house..." As the poem grew in popularity, children everywhere began to embrace the image of St. Nicholas and his flying reindeer. (Curiously, the word "Santa" is never mentioned in the book.)

The book, and later film, that has created many of our Christmas images is, of course, *A Christmas Carol,* which was published in 1843. It was there that we first met Ebenezer Scrooge, Bob Cratchit, Jacob Marley and the ghosts of Christmas

Past, Present and Future. Like the stories associated with St. Nicholas, the messages in *A Christmas Carol* are timeless: give to those in need and remember the true meaning of the season.

There have been many others, of course, who have written stories, drawn classic Christmas portraits, and who together "grew" the spirit of St. Nicholas – sometimes with more commercial results. Swedish-American artist Hans Sundblom was hired by Coca-Cola to create images for their advertising. For more than three decades, starting in 1930, Sundblom featured "Our Santa" in the Coca-Cola ads.

When the little boy in the church said "I don't get it," Santa could have explained his long lineage back to St. Nicholas. Or he could just tell him what Santa tries to *do* – and that's far more important. The spirit of Santa comes through in his actions and his presence. Santa is a representative of humility and generosity. Not all of Santa's activities can be explained, nor should they be. But, like his mentor St. Nicholas, Santa tries to emulate all that is good in this world. He tries to give freely and generously to make others happy, and does so with no expectation of anything in return. Like St. Nicholas, he is always reminded of a well-known biblical verse: "It is more blessed to give than to receive."

The modern Santa tries to convey the same message that St. Nicholas embodied more than 1,700 years ago. Rather than give gifts of monetary value, we may want to think about gifts of charity, kindness and unconditional love. In his own way, the little boy in church probably understood all of these things.

As adults we often need to be reminded.

Chapter 5
What can be done about this?

As our "sleigh" moves from party to party on a blustery afternoon in St. John's, it's hard for Santa not to see some of the contrasts. Different buildings. Different people. Different ages. Different levels of social status. Driving from a seniors home to a large corporate party can be a real head-spinner. Even after more than thirty years of Santa visits, there are always surprises.

When I arrive in the parking lot, a child with a strong voice asks his father a logical but difficult question. "Daddy, why does Santa drive a Toyota?" Luckily, his wise father has an answer. "I'll bet his sleigh is getting a final check before his big trip. He must have borrowed a truck to come and see you."

It is mid-afternoon when we are about to enter a very large golf course clubhouse where a major corporation is having a party for its employees' children. Everything is well organized by efficient elves who steer Santa towards the stage.

As I look down on the huge number of children, they are all very busy at activity sites. There is face painting and a clown making toys out of twisted balloons. There is a place where you can decorate cupcakes with every imaginable colour of icing. And there are bouncy castles and inflatable slides.

A party of this size requires a different level of toy distribution, not to mention a different level of protocol. Although Santa does have a big red chair, there are also two small chairs on either side. Children (or their parents) can choose to sit there for the photo, if that is their wish. Some concern has been expressed that children should not be expected to sit on Santa's knee anymore. Santa is fine with whatever the organizers ask. In fact, he has offered a copy of his police screening certificate prior to the event. He has also offered to sign a confidentiality agreement.

Behind Santa are two long tables piled high with gifts – most of them clearly wrapped in either pink or blue paper. The gifts are laid out in ascending order of age, starting with infants on the close end and teenagers on the far end. The corporation has purchased all these toys and has had them beautifully wrapped. There is no need for the employee parents to bring anything to this party. Elves circulate throughout the room encouraging families to go to the stage as a unit, where a professional photographer takes a group picture. Santa has set aside two hours for this event, before he has to rush off to a visit at the pediatric intensive care unit, where a family has asked for a special visit for their daughter.

Sometime during the previous summer, Mrs. Claus had issued a friendly ultimatum to Santa. *She is tired of repeating everything. Santa needs to get his hearing checked.* Well, it turns out that Mrs. Claus was right on the money. Santa has now been outfitted with new technology – and it's wonderful! Suddenly there are rediscovered sounds, especially the high-pitched treble sounds of birds and some musical notes that Santa had not been able to hear for a long time. Yes, I hear Mrs. Claus now. Everything is loud and clear.

As a result of this re-found hearing, I am drawn to a click, click, click sound on the floor. The sound is from the high heels of a seven-year-old girl who is struggling to keep her shoes on and to keep up with her sisters. Just ahead of her, there are two other girls. I'm guessing they are roughly nine and eleven. The three girls are all dressed identically. They are wearing red and green Christmas dresses; they even have the same hairstyles and bows. Then I see that they have the same watches, the same bracelets and the same necklaces. Except for the obvious age difference, they could have been triplets. Then I hear a parent giving instructions.

"Girls, go up on the stage with Santa and we will pose the photo. Don't move until I click my fingers."

A few minutes later, the elves gauge the ages of the girls, present the gifts and everything goes back to normal. Suddenly there is a commotion off to the side of the stage. The elves look a little flustered and the girls start to blush.

"My daughters opened these Barbie dolls and the dresses don't match."

Moments later, Santa is en route to the Pediatric Intensive Care Unit at the Janeway Children's Health and Rehabilitation Centre. It's only a short drive, but it feels worlds apart.

Chapter 6
And what is on Santa's wish list?

It had been a long night for them both, and Mrs. Claus was asleep when Santa got home. He had returned to the North Pole just before sunrise. He unharnessed the reindeer, put on their blankets, gave them water and some special oats and settled them into the warm stalls of the barn. They had all worked really hard and were very tired.

Santa went into the big house to fill the stockings for the elves and Mrs. Claus. Yes, their "stockings were hung by the chimney with care," just like everyone else around the world. Then Santa went to bed and fell asleep.

After a few hours of rest, Santa rolled over. This was the one morning when he and Mrs. Claus were able to sleep in. There was the smell of fresh coffee; the elves would soon be up and playing with their toys. Santa slipped out of bed and headed for the living room. He sat quietly in his big chair, thinking about all the work that had gone into the last twenty-four hours.

When he had left the Janeway Children's Health and Rehabilitation Centre in St. John's the evening before, he had gone straight to the North Pole. Everything was ready for his big trip. The whole team had done an amazing job. The sleigh was packed, the lists were checked and double-checked, and the reindeer were all hitched and anxious to go. Just before midnight, he had hugged Mrs. Claus before the big sleigh lifted off. Every year he revisited the places where people have had a profound impact on the story of Santa.

When the sleigh landed in Lycia, Turkey, he thought about the birth of St. Nicholas in 280 AD. When he dropped down from the sky in the small town of Oberndorf, Santa thought back to Christmas Eve of 1818 when *Silent Night, Holy Night* was introduced to the world. When Santa flew into New York, he thought about Clement Clarke Moore's poem *'Twas The Night Before Christmas*. And when he visited the home of Virginia O'Hanlon, he recalled her wonderful letter in 1897. In fact, he still smiles when he recalls the reply from Francis Pharcellus Church. He was the editor of the *Sun* newspaper who wrote the famous response, "Yes, Virginia, there is a Santa Claus."

Everywhere that Santa goes, he finds a wish list from children young and old. But every one of Santa's helpers has a personal wish list, too. My own wish list is about children in need. How can my work assisting Santa help with the world effort to eliminate polio, the crippling disease that still attacks children in Pakistan, Afghanistan and Nigeria. Those are the only three countries in the world where the disease is still not under control.

One of the problems is civil war. If peace could be found, then the work of Rotary International and other great organizations could finally eradicate polio.

I sit quietly in my chair as I begin to hum a little tune. I think you know the words.

> *Let there be peace on earth*
> *And let it begin with me;*
> *Let there be peace on earth,*
> *The peace that was meant to be.*
>
> *With God as our Father*
> *Brothers all are we,*
> *Let me walk with my brother*
> *In perfect harmony.*
>
> *Let peace begin with me,*
> *Let this be the moment now;*
> *With every step I take,*
> *Let this be my solemn vow:*
>
> *To take each moment and live each moment*
> *In peace eternally.*
> *Let there be peace on earth*
> *And let it begin with me.*

Remembering Richard

During one of my countless school visits, a child named Lucy asked me an unusual question.

"Santa, do you have any children?"

No, Lucy, Santa and Mrs. Claus do not have any sons or daughters, but we do know thousands of wonderful children just like you all around the world. Hardly a day goes by that I do not think of a child I have seen or held. Often the ones I think about are the same ones that readers of *The Man in the Red Suit* ask me about – because these children were in some kind of peril. Richard Osmond, for example was the little boy with the blue pyjamas and the number 32. Santa knew that Richard was from Cape Ray, Newfoundland, on the west coast and about 900 kilometres from St. John's. In the summer of 2013, Mrs. Claus and I drove to Cape Ray, where we met Richard's aunt. She worked at the lighthouse museum. She told us where we might find Richard's grave, if we ever wanted to visit the place where he was buried.

In the late spring of 2014, I drove west again in my truck. I wanted a photograph of that headstone, the monument to the little boy I had visited on Christmas Eve in 2005. Richard was three that Christmas. He had a brain tumor and was struggling to stay alive. He had fallen asleep waiting for Santa to visit. His mother and grandmother were there when Santa came into the room. His grandmother took the photo to prove to him that yes, Santa had come to visit while he was asleep. They showed him

that picture on Christmas morning. This photo is in *The Man in the Red Suit*.

I remember my first visit with Richard very clearly. A dear little child, he had his hand tucked under his chin and he wore a little Santa hat with the white tassel over his left shoulder. On his blue sports pajamas, the number 32 was sewn high on the shoulder. Richard loved sports.

Now, nine years later, I am going to visit him again. It's a long eleven-hour drive, so I have lots of time to think about life and its complications. For example, the word "widow" is used after the death of a spouse, while the word "orphan" is used after the death of one's parent. But there is no English word to describe the death of a child. Maybe that is because the death of a child is so difficult to fathom. It isn't supposed to happen. Maybe there is no word to describe the hurt and the pain following the death of a child, because it isn't part of the natural order of things. You aren't supposed to bury your own children.

Somewhere in the middle of the province, as I rounded one of the turns on the Trans-Canada Highway, I thought of the turns and the unknown roads ahead in the next Christmas season. Would Santa meet another child like Richard? Sadly, the probable answer was yes. Then I thought of the hectic pace my own children keep with *their* children. Hockey rinks never seem to close; lit soccer pitches can keep children running and kicking balls late into the evening. Add to this the demands of school and the planning of Christmas pageants, and life can become very, very busy.

At 7 p.m., I reached Cape Ray, turned off the highway and stopped the truck. In the distance, I could see the lighthouse and the silver reflection off the water as the sun moved lower in the sky. I opened the window to allow the sounds and the scents of my destination to sweep over me. The screaming seagulls moved up and down the coast looking for their last meal of the day, while the wind off the sea felt cold on my face as I breathed the salty ocean air. After a few minutes I drove up a short rise. There on the left was a cemetery with a white picket fence. I stopped again. This was my destination. I had driven 896 kilometres to visit Richard.

The latch on the gate was cold and rusty, but it released with a squeak as I entered the cemetery. It was not large, although it was well-kept with its predictable rows of crosses and headstones. There were many family names here and, as in every Newfoundland cemetery, there were stories on the grave markers telling of tragedies at sea – young men who drowned trying to sustain a family with what could be taken from the sea. Sometimes the sea, cruelly, takes back.

I stopped and looked to my right and left. Then I saw it. A black, vertical stone in the shape of a truck. When I walked over, I realized that the whole site was ringed in little metal cars and trucks. This had to be Richard's final resting place. A black wrought-iron fence surrounded the white marble chips that filled the centre of the site. It looked just like a sandbox that any young child would play in. There was even a toy tractor. I could imagine

Richard playing with it – moving the white marble chips while making roads and hills in and around his village.

I stood there for a long time. Then I turned back to my truck and headed for the hotel. Once inside, I turned up the heat before I clicked on the radio. The hockey game was about to start. Montreal was playing Toronto. Then came the familiar twang of Stompin' Toms iconic tune, "Hello out there, we're on the air, its hockey night tonight."

I couldn't stop thinking of my four-year-old friend, in his number 32 sports jersey. This seemed a fitting moment in which to pay tribute to this brave, young lad.

Good night, young Richard, and play on. All your fans are watching. We are with you still.

SANTA CLAUS OATH:
I promise to use "my" powers to create happiness, spread love and make fantasies come to life in the true and sincere tradition of the Santa Claus Legend.

Chapter 7
Can you pin your hat?

The Santa Claus Parade in St. John's, Newfoundland, happens on the last Sunday in November. For the 60,000 people who fill the downtown area, it's a pretty big deal. So I wasn't completely surprised when my office phone rang on the Tuesday before the parade. It was a mother asking if she could see me for a few minutes. She said she needed something very important that involved her son and his friends. I happily agreed to meet.

As she sat in my office, her story began to unfold. Tracy's son, William, was six years old. Three of his friends in school had recently told him there was no such thing as Santa. They claimed it was all just a big gag played on children by parents and grandparents. William came home very disappointed and confused. He asked his mother if Santa was real.

After chatting with William for a while, Tracy made a plan, but she needed Santa's help. Tracy suggested that William invite those children from his class who told him that there was no Santa to come to their house for a pizza party. Once they were

47

all together, she would suggest that the boys write a letter to Santa. So, on the appointed day the three boys came and Tracy got out a pad, pens, an envelope and a stamp. Before the party, Tracy also made a small but significant purchase of two identical items, one of which was to be included with the boys' letter.

Here is what Tracy suggested they write:

Dear Santa,

This letter comes to you from four boys in St. John's, Newfoundland, who are writing to tell you that we do not believe you are real. When we asked William's mother what we should do, she suggested that we write this letter as a test for Santa. We will look for the answer in 11 months' time, during the Santa Claus parade next November.

Your friends,
William, Jason, Patrick and Liam

Tracy took the boys' letter, attached her special purchase, and placed both in a thick envelope. The boys put the stamp in the correct corner before they walked to the Canada Post box to put it in the mail. Soon they returned, happy with their test for Santa. Not to mention the pizza.

"So, Santa," explained Tracy, "this is where I need your help. William and his friends mailed their letter eleven months ago and the parade is this Sunday. Would you help me out with the rest of my plan?"

It certainly seemed like a simple enough request. And Tracy had gone to some trouble to make her plan convincing. However, just to be sure, I made certain I had the boys' names and an understanding of where they would be on the sidewalk. I made sure Tracy was also aware of how my elf (and wife) Paula, walking in front of the float, could talk to Santa. Then I briefed Paula to make sure we knew how to find Tracy in the crowd.

On the big parade day, Santa's helicopter landed on schedule and he climbed up into his big sleigh. Once again there were more than 60,000 people, many of whom had brought non-perishable food items for the local food banks. Down Duckworth Street we went. Soon a large caramel-coloured building with brown chocolate drizzling down the sides came into view. Yes, this is the elves' favourite store. It's the Newfoundland Chocolate Company, Inc.

By this point, Santa was all set. He looked down, spotted the boys on the sidewalk, and waved. After shouting a hearty "Ho, Ho, Ho," he said, "Hello William, Patrick, Jason and Liam. Yes, Santa did get your letter and look; here is the pin you sent me at the North Pole last year! It is here in my hat."

Four astonished little jaws hit the sidewalk almost in unison. Did Santa really get their letter and the pin for his hat? Meanwhile, a happy but tearful Tracy dried her eyes with a tissue. Mission accomplished. If Santa can help keep the magic going for our children for a few more years, it's all worth the effort.

Chapter 8
Santa, can you keep our dream alive?

Sometimes Santa has to come up with practical solutions to some slightly impractical requests. That was the case when an email arrived at the North Pole from a busy lawyer friend.

"Santa, we have a dilemma," said the lawyer. "Our daughter, Hannah, is ten. She still believes in Santa, and she's asked for some new bedroom furniture for Christmas. Hannah's mother and I just got a call from the supplier, who says the shipment has arrived in St. John's – but it absolutely *must* be delivered to the house a week before Christmas. Is there anything Santa can do to get us out of this jam?"

These requests are always a challenge. They require a little quiet reflection to come up with a good solution, followed by a little magic, and ultimately a phone call at a prearranged time. But first, Santa needed some "insider" information. Things such as a birthdate, the names of favourite stuffed toys and maybe the names of the child's best friends. It's an illusion, and I can't deny it. But the results are worth it!

And so on a particular evening, Santa heads off to his basement office with bells on his right arm, while he glances at his watch to check the exact time. Moments later, a phone rings in the child's house.

"This is the North Pole calling. Is Hannah there, please?" There's a hush at the other end of the line. Then a parent's loud voice.

"Hannah, this call is for you. I think it's Santa at the North Pole." Then a tentative young voice comes on the line.

"Hello, Santa. This is Hannah."

"Hannah, Santa needs your help. I got your letter and I thank you for it. We loved the picture of your teddy Bearkovsky, and we know you had a great birthday. The sleepover sounds like it was lots of fun. Now, could you help the elves here and do Santa a little favour? The elves have just come to chat with Santa. They tell me the North Pole is full of toys and that you want some new furniture for your bedroom. Would you mind if Santa asked someone with a big truck to bring it to you in a few days so we have enough room to make more toys?"

"Oh, Santa! It would be wonderful if you could bring me my furniture. No, I don't mind if it comes a few days early," replies a very excited Hannah.

"Thank you, Hannah," Santa responds. "Say hello to your brothers Daniel and Ian, and I will try to find a special treat for your dog Buddy. And maybe we can look in the sleigh and see if we can find a baby orangutan! Good night, sweetheart."

There is a momentary silence before Santa rings the bells and hangs up the phone.

At the other end of the line, Hannah is so excited she can't get to sleep until after midnight.

There are also the small crises that arise when little ears hear things that dash their hopes. That was the theme of one mother's email about her young boy and his (almost) loss of Christmas innocence.

"Hi, Santa," said the mother. "I really need some help. My little boy, Malachy, is four. He wrote his letter to Santa and gave it to a postal worker at the parade. He is really getting worried because he hasn't had a reply. I recently took him with me to a postal outlet. While he was putting the stamps on my Christmas cards, a new customer came in with a child's letter. She asked if it was too late to send a letter to the North Pole. The employee, standing right next to my son, answered him in a loud voice.

"The cutoff date has passed, but give it to me anyway. It isn't like the letter actually goes anywhere. They only go to our head office."

Santa uttered a little "Ouch!"

"I tried to distract my son as he carefully applied the stamps. I don't know what *he* heard, but I was annoyed and worried that this incident would upset him. Later, I called the postal office to express my concern about their lack of sensitivity. Although they did say they were sorry, they claimed there was little they could do. Then I thought about you," she said.

"So, Santa, can you help me? Please call Malachy and tell him you got his letter." A few hours later, the phone rings at his house.

"Hello, Malachy, this is Santa at the North Pole. I am calling to tell you that I saw you in the Santa Claus Parade in St. John's, and I also want to thank you for your letter. The elves are packing all the toys in the big sleigh now. I'll do my very best to bring you a Battle Shell Donatello Ninja Turtle and a Lego Castle. I do thank you for asking me to remember the boys and girls in the hospital. And I am pleased that you will take some things to the food bank with your mum. You are a great little guy! Thank you and goodbye from all your friends at the North Pole!"

Chapter 9
Are you busy Christmas Eve?

"Santa, are you busy on Christmas Eve?" asked the email enquirer. You would think the answer would be an obvious "yes." But the truth is that by Christmas Eve all is well at the North Pole. You see, Mrs. Claus has everything under control.

The email was from Lynette, the executive director at the Dr. H. Bliss Murphy Cancer Centre in St. John's, where everything *cannot* be under control. It's just not possible.

Dear Santa,

We have a six-year-old who will undergo a cancer chemo treatment at 10:20 a.m. on Christmas Eve and we were wondering if you could be present with her while she undergoes her treatment.

Santa quickly consulted his schedule and realized that he could move a few other obligations around. There was no hesitation. *Of course* Santa could be with this child. How could there be a more important email during the whole Santa season?

I thought about my own family and how cancer had impacted two of my cousins' children in the past few years. My cousin Janet, in Toronto, has two sons and her youngest, Erik, was diagnosed with leukemia when he was four years old. Imagine the emotions you go through when a doctor tells you your energetic four-year-old boy has leukemia! Erik is now eight years old, and he has gone through four tough years of multiple hospital visits, tests and treatments.

Closer to home, my cousin Heather (Janet's sister) went to a doctor with her daughter, Beth, to figure out what was happening to her health. After a battery of visits and tests, the results came in. It was Hodgkin's lymphoma. She needed to start immediate chemotherapy treatment. Beth is a brave young lady. She went through all the terrible treatments and lost all of her hair. But just before Christmas she got some good news. She was declared cancer-free.

Early in December 2013, I learned that little Erik (now eight and also cancer-free) and his brother, Evan, would come to Newfoundland and stay for Christmas. Both Erik and Beth, these brave cancer survivors, would be in the same home on Christmas Eve morning.

On December 22nd, I got a call from the cancer centre to say that the child who was to be receiving the chemo treatment on the morning of the 24th had become very sick and was now in the Pediatric Intensive Care Unit. Santa was not needed at

10:20 a.m. because I would see her on Christmas Eve. And so Santa hatched a plan.

At this point I need to re-introduce readers to Santa's Elf 342, a great friend and a tremendously generous business owner. Elf 342 has assigned herself that number and she is one elf that Santa has counted on for many years. She donates the "Santa's Own Teddy Bears" that are given to special-needs children. Elf 342 is also a great friend of my cousin's family and, unknown to me, she had taken a special Christmas ornament to the family. Elf 342 knows all about Christmas trees and ornaments. In fact, she is a bit of a tree specialist.

She knew about a little lantern ornament that sends a signal to Santa to let him know everyone is ready and waiting for him to arrive. It is really useful when children are not in their usual home on Christmas Eve because it alerts Santa about where you are. On the night of December 23rd, Elf 342 took the ornament to this house, where the two boys hung it on the tree.

The next morning, Christmas Eve day, it was discovered

that one of the boys had decided to "test" the ornament to see how it worked. This caused great concern in the house. It wasn't the right time to be sending those kinds of signals to Santa, and no one knew what would happen.

On Christmas Eve morning, Santa pulled up outside the house and rang the bell. The astonished boys answered the door with a jaw-dropping pronouncement. "He found us in Newfoundland. How did he know?" Their mother wisely pointed to the ornament on the tree. For the next twenty minutes, Santa read to the boys and Beth joined us as well.

Later on Christmas Eve, in the pediatric intensive care unit, we met the very sick little girl who was suffering from cancer and had been admitted for Christmas. Her parents had no idea earlier in the week that this is where they would be for Christmas, but cancer does not take a Christmas break, even for children. Her condition was serious; the outcome in the short term was unsure. But she was resting, asleep and comfortable.

Many families are touched each day with the unexpected. But if your year has passed without major stress or worry, then quietly say thank you. You might even want to buy a teddy bear and drop it off at the local children's hospital. It will find a good home. Somebody, no matter what the age, will probably need a hug.

SANTA CLAUS OATH:
I will seek knowledge to be well versed in the mysteries
of bringing Christmas cheer and goodwill to all
the people that I encounter in my journeys and travels.

Chapter 10
Can you come to intensive care at 5 p.m.?

At 5 p.m. we are heading for our third visit of the after-noon as the sleigh pulls into the Janeway Children's Health and Rehabilitation Centre. As many readers will know, this is the hospital for children in Newfoundland and Labrador. The building is part of the Health Sciences Centre, the largest hospital in the province.

Santa climbs out of the sleigh and walks through the auto-matic doors of the Janeway entrance. There is no need for us to go through emergency, because we are here today for a very spe-cial visit. As we walk into the hospital, the long walls of beautiful murals greet us. There are teddy bears and elephants, giraffes and lions, all with big smiles for everyone who passes by. In the centre of the atrium, where the hallways meet, there is a large boat where children can play and peek through portholes to forget for just a moment that they are actually in the hospital. The whole building is designed to let children act…. well, like children.

When the large elevator doors open, we push the button for the fourth floor. The elevator has doors and buttons on both sides. In fact, it is large enough to accept a full-length bed. When the elevator doors open, we walk to the medical unit where Santa is greeted by the nurses. They have been expecting him. My little friend has been removed from her room and is dressed, sitting in a wheelchair. Her parents are there once again, as is her sister, Callie.

A decision has been made to take her home, so Santa has been asked to visit this wonderful little girl who has been seriously sick for a couple of months. Those of you who read the earlier book will know Chelsea as the child who had a seizure and was unconscious for fifteen hours on Christmas Eve – at least until Santa arrived that evening and rang his bells. It was Chelsea's mother who described the scene as being the "real magic of Christmas and Santa."

Since then, Chelsea has had some ups and downs. But in the fall of 2012, Chelsea's medical condition deteriorated. The family was told that Chelsea's spine had an eighty-degree curve in it. The bones would soon start to crush the organs on one side of her body. Without major surgery to put two metal telescopic rods on either side of her spine, she would only live another two to three years.

If that was not bad enough, doctors were not even sure if Chelsea's little body, already medically fragile, could tolerate the twelve-hour surgery. And the surgery would have to be done by specialists in Montreal. Happily, Chelsea made it through the surgery, but after a few setbacks she was transferred back to St. John's. These were long days. Chelsea had to be turned every few hours. She required high doses of morphine for the pain. Soon, she developed infections, became dehydrated and had to cope with about twenty seizures a day.

By this time it was mid-December. A combination of tubes, monitors, needles, tests, medications and intravenous hookups quickly erased any thought of even a remotely "normal" Christmas for this family. And this is why Santa had been asked to come to the hospital. The family could not conceive of "celebrating" Christmas. How could they be joyous at Christmas while their little Chelsea was so sick? All they wanted was to bring Chelsea home. Nothing else mattered anymore – just keeping Chelsea medically stable enough to get her home, eventually.

Santa has visited Chelsea for many years, and she always seemed to respond to his bells. As in the past, Santa would go over to Chelsea, get close enough so she could feel his beard against her face, and then he would take her limp hand in his and give the bells a little jingle. Nothing, but then a little smile from Chelsea, and another one from her mom, another from her dad, and a giggle from her one-year-old sister, Callie. Could there be enough magic in Santa's bells for this family to feel the Christmas spirit again?

After a few minutes, Chelsea seemed tired. She was having a hard time staying awake. As the medical staff looked on, Santa took a teddy bear out of his mailbag. There couldn't be a better place for "Santa's Own Teddy Bear" than to be with Chelsea at Christmas.

In mid-January 2013, a letter arrived at the North Pole. Chelsea is non-verbal, so Santa and Mrs. Claus have received a number of letters written through her mother, Kim.

Dear Santa,

There are just not enough "thank yous." My mom and dad are overwhelmed with gratitude for everything you have done for me and my family. This year past, they had totally cancelled Christmas because they thought they didn't have the time or the energy to pull it off…..

So thank you Santa, for putting my mom and dad back in the Christmas Spirit (again!)

Chelsea

During the Christmas season, Santa goes on many journeys. Many of them are journeys of the heart. All of them teach me something. Chelsea's journey was no different. Experts tell us to "nourish our children." But maybe, just maybe, they are the ones who nourish us.

Chapter 11
Santa, can you dance Gangnam Style?

In the three weeks leading up to the children's Flight to the North Pole, one child is selected for the trip each morning on live radio. The children are chosen based on a question that they would like to ask Santa, in person, in the North Pole. The questions are read out over the air. Then the station calls the child live on the radio with the news that they have been selected for this memorable adventure. Sometimes the radio is on in the North Pole, so we get to hear the broadcast.

Some of those questions have actually sent Santa scurrying to the library or to his keyboard for Google assistance. There have been some pretty tricky ones. "Why are there are only eight reindeer in *'Twas the Night Before Christmas,* and where was Rudolph?" That was almost a stumper. But the *real* stumpers are the ones where I have to do something athletic or rhythmic.

One day in the fall of 2012 I was walking downtown when some business people I knew waved and laughed. Some of them stopped me on the sidewalk and asked if I could dance Gangnam Style. I couldn't figure out what they were talking about! I had never heard the words before. Mrs. Claus, of course, is quite convinced that I live back in the Dark Ages, when the limbo and the twist were in vogue. (If the reader doesn't know about these dance styles, you'll have to ask your parents or grandparents.)

The next morning, when I turned on the Steele Communications Hits FM 99.1 radio show, host Randy Snow was very excited about Sarah's question for Santa. He told listeners to stay tuned for a replay of her interesting question. Apparently he was repeating what people had asked me on the street.

"Santa, Sarah wants to know if you can dance Gangnam Style?"

Like every good Neanderthal male, I'm in the dark when it comes to dance moves. I had to ask Mrs. Claus.

"What is Gangnam Style?" Of course, that just made her laugh.

"You haven't heard Psy on the radio. Do you live under a rock?"

Off I went to work with Santa's outfit in my suitcase, feeling a little sheepish. Later that day, Santa got prepared for the children's hospital's annual concert and sing-along. This is always a special day. Children who can walk do so, and others in wheelchairs and striker-frames are brought along by helpers. They all gather in the atrium, where doctors and nurses dressed as clowns join local actors to bring a few hours of fun into the world of ailing children. It is wonderful to hear the children laugh when the doctors and nurses perform skits and dress up as odd characters. Here are the people who were putting needles in them this morning and now they are here having fun! How cool is that?

After the concert has finished and the children are taken back to their rooms, Santa's wonderful Elf Margaret from the Janeway Children's Health and Rehabilitation Centre turns and catches me off guard.

"Well, Santa, can you dance Gangnam Style or not? You only have three days to learn before the big flight."

Santa must have looked confused and dejected. Soon the candy stripers from child physiotherapy show up.

"Okay, Santa. Come this way." Three of them march Santa down a corridor and push open a conference room door. One of the students boots up her iPod and the next thing I hear is a pounding beat coming from a small speaker.

"Come here, Santa. Stand next to us and follow these moves." Then, with two arms folded over at the wrist and my body moving in time to what sounds like music, I join my student elves in the basics of Gangnam Style. Psy might not have approved, but my student-nurse friends soon give Santa a thumbs up and a passing grade. His moves will be good enough that he can have fun with the children on the plane. (If only he can remember all those moves three days later!)

On Saturday morning, we turn on the radio at 6:30 a.m. at the North Pole. The announcer says he has talked to the elves at the airport and the children are arriving before going through security. I roll out of bed, stumble into the shower, and try to wake up. As I stand in the hot steam, I cross my left and right wrists and start to move around under the steaming hot water. So far, so good. Now only one more hour to go.

Soon, we are at an airport hangar, standing in the cold morning sunshine waiting for the arrival of Provincial Airlines Flight number HO HO HO. It lands exactly on time at 7:30 a.m. Santa walks to the plane just as the engines are shut down and the stairs unfold from the fuselage. It is snowing heavily, so Santa is soon covered in white flakes. Up the steps I go with a bound. I open the curtain into the passenger area and look at the over-joyed faces of children jumping up and down shouting.

"Santa, Santa!"

First things first. Santa has to do this dance, so he can stop fretting about it. He calls out to a little girl in row six.

"Sarah, do you still want to dance Gangnam Style with Santa?" The little girl leaps out of her seat and comes rushing forward. The amazing technicians from the airline and the radio station have arranged to pipe Psy and his Korean band through the speakers on the plane. Pretty soon the place is alive. Not only are Sarah and Santa dancing Gangnam Style, but all of the children are soon on their feet. The whole plane is rocking!

Apparently Santa still has a few moves left in him, despite the long white beard. I guess if he can shimmy up and down all those chimneys…

Chapter 12
May I think about that one?

Santa really has to pluck up his courage when he is part of a live and unrehearsed event – especially when children are firing rapid questions at him. Who knows what the heck they are going to ask? I suppose the parents and grandparents are sitting in hesitant wonder, too. Their greatest fear is that a child will reveal some horrible family secret, or ask a particularly embarrassing question. Oh, the innocence of children.

The only thing more challenging is if Santa is on live television for a two-hour call-in show. That is a *really* big deal. There is a studio host and a whole army of camera people and technical personnel ready to connect with the children. The show is advertised for weeks beforehand, and the switchboard lights up like the proverbial Christmas tree once the phone number appears on the home television screen. The studio is also *very* warm. There are bright lights beaming down on Santa as he sits in a big red chair. (But Santa is comfortable thanks to the blue frozen freezer bags stuffed into his big belly!)

The program is divided into segments, which run about nine minutes each, followed by a one-minute break. It's just enough time to take a drink of water, but not enough time for Santa to run to a washroom. (Santa has been very careful of his liquid intake in the hours prior to the show.) One year, an inquisitive child cheerfully asks a simple question.

"Santa, what is the last thing you do before you leave the North Pole on Christmas Eve?"

Now, I really do want to say that Santa goes to the bathroom! But I think that is a bit too much information. So I settle for something slightly more endearing.

"Santa kisses Mrs. Claus goodbye, and he waves to the elves as the reindeer lift the heavy sleigh into the sky."

The live call-in show is going smoothly. Over time, Santa is getting used to following the red lights on top of the three studio cameras, which come on to indicate the one that is active. There are monitors that Santa and the host can see, and the names of the children and their location come up on the screen just prior to the child connecting through the studio sound system. With the technology of global satellites and web-connected computers, children can be phoning from almost anywhere, so it is not unusual for the host to turn to Santa to offer some commentary.

"Santa, our next callers are Zoe, age six, and Jason, age four. They are calling from Fort McMurray, Alberta. Say hi to Santa, Zoe and Jason."

Once Santa has traded greetings and asked about the weather in Fort McMurray, or the name of their favourite hockey team, we get down to business and ask what the two callers would like for Christmas. Zoe needs a new hockey stick, while Jason asks for an Elf on the Shelf. Both ask that Santa remember the children who will be in the hospital on Christmas Eve, which is very thoughtful. Santa assures them he will be able to see all of the children.

It might have been wise to stop right there, but Santa really puts his foot in it, so to speak. He asks if they have any questions, and Jason says he does.

"Santa, our Grampie told us that the reindeer had left a big mess in our back yard," said Zoe. "But when Jason and I went out to make a snowman, it looked like a chocolate bar to us. We asked our Grampie, and he said that it was definitely left there on Christmas Eve. So we need to know if your magic reindeer poop chocolate?"

Well, there is a look of panic on the host's face. I think she is all set to hit the "bleep" button or go to a commercial break to give Santa thirty seconds to come up with a good answer. But this is live television. Zoe needs an immediate answer from Santa.

It's a good thing that the spirit of St. Nicholas is never far from Santa. He always seems to come through in a pinch. Santa takes a deep breath, looks into the camera, and out comes the answer.

"Aha! So your house was where we dropped the candy bar! Santa has a snack box in his sleigh. When we were flying over Fort McMurray, Dasher handed Santa a candy bar and I dropped it. Now I know where it landed!"

"Thank you, Santa," I hear Jason chime in. "We will tell our Grampie it was just one of your chocolate bars. He'll be glad to know the magic reindeer are feeling fine."

Here's a plea to all the Grampies out there who wish to keep the Christmas dream alive for children: Please give me a heads-up when you're going to throw me a curve-ball. I'm a good catcher – but I'm not getting any younger!

Remembering Ariel

Those of you who read *The Man in the Red Suit* will remember Ariel Langdon. There is a full-colour picture of her with Santa in the Pediatric Intensive Care Unit on page 140. Sadly, you'll also know that she passed away shortly after Santa's visit. I got close to several families as the first book was being written, because you can't include details about children's lives – not to mention their photos – without the consent of the parents. All of those memories came back several months later in September of 2012 when I was at the launch for my book.

On the one hand, I was enjoying the chance to meet and talk to so many friends and Santa supporters. It was quite an experience. I sat at a table with a box of red pens and a mountain of books, while people stood in a long line waiting to have their copy signed. You have to write quickly, but you also want to give some personal attention to everyone who has come to the event. I was focused on the book in my hand when I happened to look up. There stood Krista Langdon, Ariel's mother. I looked at Krista with a lump in my throat, not sure what to say.

"How should I sign your book?" I managed to say, trying not to get choked up.

Krista looked at me and answered, *"To my future baby brother or sister. Love, Ariel."* Somehow I was able to steer my red pen as I tried to focus through the watery blur in my eyes.

In December of 2012, Krista sent me a lovely Christmas card with the comforting poem, "Christmas in Heaven," by Wanda Bencke. She apparently penned the poem as her daughter, Lysandra Kay Bencke, lay in a coma for five days. She wrote it to show Lysandra's excitement at being in Heaven – while also being keenly aware of the heartache and sadness her family was experiencing on Earth.

Christmas in Heaven

I see the countless Christmas trees
Around the world below
With tiny lights, like heaven's stars
Reflecting on the snow
The sight is so spectacular
Please wipe away that tear
For I'm spending Christmas
With Jesus Christ this year
I hear the many Christmas songs
That people hold so dear
But the sounds of music can't compare
With the Christmas choir up here
For I have no words to tell you
The joy their voices bring
For it is beyond description
To hear an angel sing
I can't tell you of the splendor
Or the peace here in this place
Can you just imagine Christmas
With our Savior face to face?
I'll ask Him to light your spirit
As I tell Him of your love
So then pray for one another

As you lift your eyes above
Please let your heart be joyful
And let your spirit sing
For I'm spending Christmas in Heaven
And I'm walking with the King!

by Wanda Bencke copyright 1997
name changed to Wanda White in 2010

SANTA CLAUS OATH:
I shall be dedicated to hearing the secret
dreams of both children and adults.

Chapter 13
Can you bring back my puppy?

As we saw in an earlier chapter, the flight to the North Pole is a very special adventure for children. It's also a big challenge for Santa, although he has lots of helpers. Before the flight begins, the elves at Provincial Airlines have sent the flight manifest to Santa, so he knows where every child is seated. He also knows the question that each child wants Santa to answer.

I remember one child with a *special* request. It was going to test St. Nicholas and draw on the wisdom of Santas throughout the ages. The question came in a letter rolled and tied in a bow and handed to Santa by a child. Luckily, Santa knew the letter was coming. Here's what it said:

Dear Santa,

I hope that you are having a good Christmas at the North Pole. Only reason why I am giving you this letter is because I want to tell what I want for Christmas. It is only one thing. I know it might be a lot but here is what it is. It is my dog Buddy, he got sick and died. If you can use your magic and bring Buddy back, please do so as it would mean the world to me.

Love, Samantha

Santa picked up Samantha and gave her a big hug as she handed over her letter. I told her I already knew what was in her letter – and I had some news for her. I explained that all the elves had special helpers who did extra chores at the North Pole. In fact, I told her Buddy was with all the other kittens and puppies. In fact, he was probably playing with Rudolph right now. I asked her if she would mind if Buddy stayed with us in the North Pole. Did she think she and her mummy could find another puppy? Slowly, she released her tight grip on Santa's neck as she turned to her mother.

"Mummy, Santa wants Buddy to stay here in the North Pole with him, with Mrs. Claus and all the elves. I told him that was a wonderful idea, and maybe you and I could find another puppy." Her mother gave me the thumbs-up sign.

Then I took one of Santa's Own Teddies from my mailbag. I explained to Samantha that I had very special teddy bears with their own little red scarves.

"These teddies are given to very special children. If you will give Teddy a new home in your house, I'm sure Teddy will be very happy with you."

"Thank you, Santa," Samantha replied. "You look after Buddy and I will look after Teddy."

St. Nicholas might be able to do miracles and bring people and animals back to life. Santa just does the best he can with his less-than-divine powers – and his numerous helpers.

Chapter 14
Santa, can you help me stop smoking for Christmas?

The planes they use to ferry passengers back and forth between St. Pierre and St. John's are pretty small. Even a Santa of my size has to duck his head as he boards. The seats are a tight squeeze, too. On one of these flights, the woman seated next to me seemed a little apprehensive as the big six-blade propeller started to spin just outside the window. Soon, we pushed back and I settled in for the thirty-seven-minute flight at a relatively low altitude of 15,000 feet. I was about to start reading a book for the short-hop flight when the woman next to me turned sideways.

"You wrote a Santa book, didn't you?" I was surprised to be recognized in the middle of summer, and I had never met my seat companion before.

"Yes, I did," I replied.

Apparently she had read it and given it to others. She said that it must be quite a privilege to visit the children in the hospital on Christmas Eve, although she suspected some of the visits must be very difficult. I asked about her family and learned that she had two children and three grandchildren. When I enquired about her trip to St. John's, she told me she had a medical appointment for her lungs. You could hear the rasp in her breathing; she didn't have to tell me she was a heavy smoker. After we chatted some more, she opened her purse. She unzipped several compartments and took out the pictures of a little boy and a slightly older little girl.

"These children are the joy of my life," she said. "I love to be with them every chance I get." We talked some more about her plans for Christmas and what she might do with her grandchildren. Then she offered some more information, but very quietly.

"I told you I had three grandchildren. My daughter had another little girl, but it was stillborn." She opened another zippered compartment. This time she took out a picture of an infant in a little red hat.

"They let us take one picture before the funeral of our grandchild. She died on Christmas Eve. Here is the picture taken with Santa."

There was a long stretch of silence before I could reply.

"And what could Santa bring you for Christmas?" I asked. She looked at me with tears in her eyes.

"Santa, can you help me stop smoking?"

Well, that is a request you don't get every day! So I asked her to think about some event that might happen in fifteen or twenty years – some special occasion she would want to attend. She thought for a moment before replying.

"The marriage of my grandchildren."

I told her I was no expert on smoking or any other addiction. However, I once heard five words change a person's addiction to alcohol. I remember it was on a CBC Radio program, and the person being interviewed was explaining what he had done to overcome his addiction. The answer, he said, was to *"find something you love more."*

I know many people to whom I have said those words. Usually, they make people stop and think. They imagine their children and grandchildren, and how they want loved ones to remember them in the future. But even more important, they realize how their addiction has been clouding their own ability to remember the laughter of the children and the experiences of those they loved growing up.

So, I encouraged the lady in the seat next to me to try something. When I asked her where she kept her cigarettes, she opened a beautiful silver cigarette case with her initials engraved on the cover. The cigarettes were on one side, with the lighter on the other. I asked her to take out the lighter and to put the pictures of her grandchildren in the cigarette case. At first she said she couldn't do that to her grandchildren's pictures. But then we chatted a bit longer. Then she slowly put the pictures in and snapped the case shut. We agreed that the journey without smoking would be a difficult one. We also agreed that she might need professional help. However, if she focused on "something she loved more" and she looked at the children's pictures every time she opened the cigarette case, then surely she could increase her chances of being at her grandchildren's weddings.

Soon the plane's engines changed their pitch as we started our descent. The pilot came over the intercom, while the big doors opened under the wing and the wheels dropped down to lock for our landing. After the plane touched down, we taxied to the gate. Soon we were going through Immigration and Customs together. Before we departed, she asked if I was coming back to her island home. I said it was quite likely I would return. Then she asked if I would call her so she could tell me how she was doing. I was happy to agree.

Then, with a twinkle in her eye, she asked if she was still on Santa's good list. Either way, she was certain he would be there for her grandchildren on Christmas Eve. She wished me well in the hospital on Christmas Eve, before she gave me a big hug.

"Thank you, Santa, for coming for me today. I will never forget this day as long as I live."

Chapter 15
Can you make the not-so-normal seem normal again?

In earlier parts of this book, I have used the terms illusion, magic, and even miracle. The illusions are used to keep the dream alive for children. We do whatever is necessary in order to make children's dreams come true. Illusions are things like a magician's trick, which can be easily explained. Magic is more like a feeling that is sometimes present in a room. It's a special moment that often happens on Christmas Eve in the children's hospital. You can sense it in this letter from Alice as she writes to Santa about his visit with her son Graysen.

Dearest Santa,

It has taken me days to write this, as I have been trying to put how you made me and my family feel (two years in a row) into words, realizing we only get one opportunity to describe one family's experience on Christmas Eve. I could write a whole book on the joy and peace you spread.

When I found out we were expecting our fourth child, I was over the moon. After having three beautiful girls, deep down I longed for a boy. After nineteen long weeks of waiting, we arrived at our first ultrasound, so anxious to catch a glimpse of the little miracle inside. In an instant my whole world turned upside down. I was told that my baby had some complications and we were referred to genetics. The very next day my husband Steve and I met with genetics and we were told that the ultrasound findings compared to those of a child with Down's syndrome or that of a chromosomal issue with chromosome 18, which was fatal. I was told that if I was able to carry our baby to term, the child might last a few days, a few weeks, but we certainly would not celebrate their first birthday. I was numb.

We went to the maternal fetal assessment unit, where they did an amniocentesis. We then met with social workers and psychiatrists to decide "what we were going to do" about the situation. Being a person who is very in tune with my faith, I decided I wasn't going to do anything about anything. If God decided he wanted to do something about this, well that was entirely up to Him! So we continued to go to ultrasounds week after week for the following seventeen weeks. Some weeks were terrible, finding new complications. Other weeks seemed a little more positive.

Then finally ALL the results were in from the amnio. It was not Down's syndrome OR the chromosome 18 issue! But we were still unsure what was going on inside. Finally, on October 3rd 2012, at 11:43 a.m., and weighing in at 5 lbs, 9 oz, Graysen Thomas Power was born! I never knew a thing until they whisked him off to the NICU, where

I later got to meet him. He had some complications at birth, so they had to give him a breathing tube right away. The next day they were able to remove the breathing tube, but he still needed a little bit of support. Blood tests were sent off to see what was happening.

He was then diagnosed, six weeks later, with a rare genetic syndrome called Cornelia de Lange syndrome. On top of CdLS, he also had chronic lung disease. So we stayed in NICU, and stayed, and stayed, and before I knew it, it was Christmas – a time of year I have always enjoyed more than anything else in this world, until that year. Although I had three other children at home who also love Christmas as much as I always did, having a child in hospital just killed me! I honestly didn't care if Christmas came at all that year.

Knowing that my husband would be returning home for Christmas (he works away on rotation work), I thought this might brighten my spirits a little. It helped, but I was still struggling with trying to put on a happy face. It's a lot harder than it looks to pretend your whole world is not crashing down around you for the sake of your children. So, after my husband returned home and we decorated the house, I was feeling a little better, until a few days before Christmas.

There had been a chicken pox scare in our room in the NICU, and we were placed on isolation procedures. This meant that only parents were able to visit their babies. We had to gown up, wear masks and put on gloves. The staff was unable to receive admissions to our room, but they could discharge a baby throughout the isolation procedures. That part didn't bother me. What bothered me was that my girls weren't able to see their baby brother on Christmas Day. The little bit of happiness I had managed to reserve was deflated from the balloon I called life.

Then the big night came, Christmas Eve, the night of all nights. My absolute favourite night since I was a small child, and I had to pull myself out of bed that morning. I decided I really had to make an effort, not only because it was Graysen's first Christmas, but for the three beautiful darlings I have at home, who knew nothing of what was going on. They didn't understand why their brother wasn't home to share in the celebrations, and if he had to be in hospital, why weren't they allowed to see him? I felt like my heart was going to explode.

Later in the evening, Steve and I decided it would be a good idea to go in and spend some time with our little man. We arrived at the NICU, suited up, and went in for a visit. Because only discharges could occur, there was only Graysen and a sweet little baby girl in our room that night. A little while later we heard Santa's bells! The little girl that really wasn't lost in me jumped up and ran to the doorway!

"Oh my goodness, it's SANTA!"

Our nurse for the evening said that yes, indeed, Santa comes every year and visits every child at the Janeway! Hoooooray!! Finally something to look forward to. Then one of Santa's elves came in to explain the situation.

"Unfortunately, Santa will not be able to visit in here this evening due to the isolation precautions."

I burst into tears; the only thing I had looked forward to in months was not going to happen. I cried for over an hour until I had nothing left in me. So we stayed for a little longer. Then, realizing the time, not wanting to leave because a baby's first Christmas should not be this way, I decided if I was getting out of bed at all the next day, we should probably get on the move. As I was putting Graysen back to bed, the door to Graysen's room slid open and lo and behold, Santa was standing in front of us!

Our nurse said, "Oh Santa, we didn't think you were coming." Santa simply looked up and beamed.

"Santa comes to visit EVERYBODY!!!!!"

I was so happy! I think I had forgotten what it was like to be so happy. Santa stayed for quite a while, rocking both Graysen and his darling little roommate in the rocking chair next to their cribs, singing to them. Then, when the tears stopped streaming down my face, we all posed for some pictures.

In the half-hour that Santa visited our precious little ones, I had forgotten how upset I was. He made the not-so-normal seem normal for just a little while. Although I knew we had a rough road ahead, those moments with Santa seemed to erase all the sadness that had been consuming me, even for just a short time. Graysen went on to stay in hospital for a few months after our visit from Santa. Finally, on the 21st of March, 2013, we took our little man home for the first time. We were finally one big happy family!!

We were chugging along quite magically until the 27th of May when I had to bring him into the Janeway emergency department with increased oxygen requirements. Two days later we were rushed to the PICU, where we were thrown into a life-or-death situation. I had to call my husband home from Labrador because the doctors told me they were very unsure if Graysen was going to make it! Thankfully after a long stressful time, Graysen did in fact come out of it and returned home on the 11th of July.

There have been three more PICU stays since that dreadful one in May, but never as serious. The last admission was on the 12th of December of 2013. Here we were again, round two of Christmas at the Janeway. And in walks Santa! I could feel the tingle in my toes.

Graysen was sound asleep. Santa went over to talk to him, rang the bells, but Graysen continued to sleep peacefully. So Santa stayed for some pictures and a little chat.

Just when I thought he was off to visit the next little child somewhere out there in the Janeway, he plopped himself down in a rocking chair and sat ME down on his knee! Santa rocked me, sang to me, and reminded me of what a great job I was doing. He then asked me if it would be okay to share Graysen's story in his next book "because he is a very special little boy."

Then Santa reached down into his sack and produced a teddy bear that read "Santa's Own Bear 2013."

I've never cried happier tears in my life!

Alice

SANTA CLAUS OATH:
I acknowledge that some of the requests I will hear
will be difficult and sad. I know in these difficulties there
lies an opportunity to bring a spirit of warmth,
understanding and compassion.

Chapter 16
What can Santa bring you?

Early in November, the North Pole got a call asking if Santa could come to a very special birthday party for a senior who was going to be 102 years old. When the day arrived, the weather was crisp. The exhaust from cars in the parking lot emitted white smoke, and the snow crunched under Santa's big black boots. Children took their parents' hands as they rushed into the warm building to see grandparents and great-grandparents. Everywhere you looked there were bags of gift-wrapped boxes and presents. Santa skipped along through the snow with the children. We even threw a few snowballs.

In the reception area, Santa was greeted by a staff member dressed all in red with a sprig of holly in her hair.

"This way, Santa," my elf directed. Then, just inside the main door, a sprightly senior started down a long hallway toward us. The caregiver gave me the resident's first name and told me she was their newest arrival.

"She is wonderful and young at heart for her ninety-two years."

She certainly seemed bright and happy. In fact she was singing "Santa Claus is Coming to Town" as she tottered toward us. Her walker had a garland of tinsel wrapped around it. A button fixed to the right handle turned on some flashing Christmas lights. As she approached, her face broke into an impish grin.

"Santa, can I have a hug?" Then, to my surprise, she left her walker and came forward with her arms extended. I squeezed tight, tucking her head under my chin. After a few moments I let her go and asked a now-familiar question.

"And what can Santa bring you for Christmas, my dear?"

She leaned forward and said, "Let me whisper in your ear." Then, in a flirty voice, she leaned close to me.

"Any chance I can go on a date with Santa on Christmas Eve?"

Well, that was a new one for Santa! Luckily the attendant took the elderly soul's arm and steered her back to her walker before I had to reply.

"Come, Santa, the birthday lady is this way."

So we went to the elevator and got out on the third floor, which was marked "Assisted Living." As we exited onto the floor, Santa looked left and right down the long hallway. Some of the doors had cheery Christmas cards attached to them. Some had decorations and lights flickering. Music and laughter came from many of the rooms as children and grandchildren delighted their senior relatives.

We went into the room of a senior who I recognized as a

former broadcaster with a local radio station. He used to host call-in shows for several hours late at night. People called in from all over Newfoundland to ask his advice on how they should solve a problem. This man had the patience of Job, the wisdom of Solomon and a marvelous sense of humour. So Santa thought he would be a good person to consult.

"There is a lady on the floor below who wants to go on a date with Santa. What should I do?" I asked. He looked at me with a twinkle in his eyes.

"What room is she in, Santa? Let me borrow your hat!"

I roared with laughter, while my elf assistant took our photo together. Soon we came to a plain door at the end of the hall. Before we entered, my staff elf turned and indicated that their guest was barely responsive today.

"This guest is all alone. Her husband died thirty years ago when he was seventy-two. Her son and daughter died when they were in their seventies. There are no grandchildren. Her brothers and sisters have all predeceased her. So she is truly all by herself. We are all she has."

As we gently opened the door, we called her name. Then we entered the room with a jingle of the bells and a "Ho, Ho, Ho." The candy stripers joined us as we stood around the bed. This very weak senior was lying on her side with her eyes open but staring blankly ahead. Her thin hands had what looked like a layer of dry parchment skin over a bony frame. Blood vessels and bruises were visible. Her chin and cheekbones were visible; her breathing was shallow. I watched as a caregiver ran a brush through her thin gray hair. When one of the staff touched our elderly guest, she slowly turned toward me.

"Oh, Santa," she said in a very weak voice. "It is kind of you to come."

"Happy Birthday," Santa replied. "And many more may you see."

A cupcake was produced with a single candle, but the dear soul was too weak to blow it out. So we all blew together and sang "Happy Birthday." Then, Santa approached the bed, got inches away from the dear lady's face, held her frail hands and asked his favourite question.

"And what can Santa bring for you this Christmas?"

She looked back at me and answered.

"Santa, just bring me home to the Lord, my son. I am all ready to go."

A caregiver put a straw in a tiny glass of sherry and moved it to her lips. She tried to suck from it, but with no success. So the caregiver took a napkin, dipped it in the sherry, and touched it to the woman's dry lips. This brought a smile. Then I leaned forward to kiss her on the cheek. All I could say was that Santa would do his best. And as I left the room, I realized I wasn't even sure what "best" would mean in this context.

Perhaps just listening to her wish was all I could do.

Chapter 17
Santa, do you hear squitters?

Sometimes a call to Santa's office gets off on the wrong foot. I know the *intentions* are usually good, but the *tone* of the questions isn't always on the mark.

"Are you the man who plays Santa?" someone will ask. Or the caller will be misguided about what I do, or how I do it.

"I hear you have a great costume. Do you rent it out?" Those of you who know me won't be surprised at my answers to these and similar questions.

"No, I don't *play* Santa. No, you can't *rent* my suit. I do know Santa well and I can arrange for him to visit. Now how can I help you?"

As you can imagine, Santa's suit is a one-of-a-kind outfit. In fact, it gets updated about every ten years when the multiple dry-cleanings and the spray dyes on the belts and gloves require these parts to be replaced. Fortunately, Santa has some wonderful elf tailors. These long red coats with white fur trim need to be flawless, so "replacement" suits take time and money to create. There is another benefit of this Santa inventory, and readers will soon understand the wisdom of keeping Santa's wardrobe freshly dry-cleaned and waiting to be called into service. Sometimes there are completely unexpected events and even "accidents." At these times, Santa has to be ready to get back into action.

One time when Santa was asked to visit a daycare, I arrived to find that the facility was in the basement of a senior citizens' home. The visit with the children was to happen at 10 a.m., after which we would see the seniors. When Santa arrived at the daycare, the room was full of young children, as well as some mothers with infants still in their car-seats and carriers. On this occasion, Santa approached a mother to ask if he could carry the child. The mother was quick to reply.

"Of course, Santa, but be careful because my son is a little off today." Well, the little guy seemed great to me, so I picked him up and went off for a visit with the daycare children and the seniors. The mother came along, too. A few minutes into Santa's adventure, the child's face went red. There was gurgle in the diaper. Then there was a familiar but pungent odour. The mother seemed a little embarrassed.

"Oh, Santa, he has the squitters. I told you he was a little off today." Santa assured the mother this was nothing new; he was ready for any occasion. She didn't know that accidents are anticipated. Hundreds of children have sat on Santa's knee over the years, so there have been many times when excitement has led to an incident. Every Santa has to be ready, because the next event could be in less than an hour's time. First, I have to head to the big red suitcase in the sleigh. There I will find a second pair of red pants, just in case. Happily on this occasion, the replacement pants were not necessary.

Santa returned the child to the mother and off they went to the change room. Santa then turned his focus to the children who were all reading a book together while lying on the floor. When I looked up, the elf organizer gave me a signal: we needed to head off to see the seniors. At this point, the children helped Santa get up as he waved goodbye to everyone.

The seniors' portion of the building is on multiple storeys and levels, which correspond with the level of care needed by the client. We usually start with the level three guests. These are the people who simply seek the amenities of home because they are tired or lonely, and the chores of snow clearing and house maintenance are beyond them. Medically, they are in good shape; they don't require a lot of special care.

Santa has a visit with every senior. We laugh and joke about their recollections of early Christmas memories in outport Newfoundland, and how they went mummering door-to-door when they were young.

Level two is usually on a different floor. Here you will see more staff and professionals working with the residents. There may be the occasional nurse on this level, with increased services available as needed. You see more walkers, pill trays and food trays carried into rooms – as opposed to the clients in the central dining room who need less personal attention. (You might see a slightly shaky hand from Parkinson's disease, but most residents seem cheerful and happy.) Free access is allowed on levels two and three, where the residents know how to navigate the floor and the building. Again, Santa has a great visit. We chat about the photos of grandchildren and the cards which adorn their walls. It is generally a happy time.

Then we move to the nursing floor, where the elf attendant swipes an access card through the reader to gain access. Everything here is different. As soon as we enter the Assisted Living floor, I am struck by the smell of disinfectant and strong cleaning supplies. The elf takes Santa from room to room, although I'm not sure what I will find behind each door. Advanced Alzheimer's and other dementias are crippling diseases for some of these seniors. Knuckles and hands are swollen with arthritis; backs are twisted with dowager's humps and osteoporosis.

All of this seems bearable when the mind is sharp, but that's not the case with everyone on this floor. Sometimes I see empty frames of bodies – patients staring blankly at wide-screen televisions with their eyes half-closed and their mouths open. The attendant will shake the resident's arm and say loudly, "Santa is here to see you." Sometimes there is a response. Despite the sound of the bells on Santa's arm, sometimes there is no response at all.

We go into a dark room where the curtains are drawn. As Santa approaches the bedside where this very elderly senior is resting, there is a gurgling sound and a sigh of relief. Then I detect the same odour I smelled less than an hour before in the day-care.

"Oh, Santa, I am sorry. I believe our guest has the squitters."

I shake my head to indicate this is all fine. I kiss the dear soul on the cheek. Then, with the assistant's help, I take a lemon sucker and put it on the woman's lips. She licks it quietly – and we leave the room.

We are frail as we enter the world. And sometimes we are equally frail as we make our exit from it.

Chapter 18
Is Santa coming today to PICU?

Early in December of each year, Santa starts his visits to the Janeway Children's Health and Rehabilitation Centre in St. John's. We start with a photo visit for the little ones in the Neonatal Unit and the children in Pediatric Intensive Care Unit. There might be thirty or forty babies in the nursery and NICU, but each one is brought to Santa. I sit in a rocking chair near a decorated tree for this special occasion. To keep all the details straight, a hospital photographer and a staff person with a clipboard match the child's hospital armband number with the photo numbers. Near Santa on the wall is a hand sanitation unit where my big white gloves are sprayed to make them germ-free between every child.

Sometimes the family members are present, which adds to the fun. Sometimes there are twins. And sometimes children are brought attached to IV poles or oxygen apparatus. This gets a bit complicated. But sometimes the children are just incredibly small, and I marvel at the strength of their will to survive.

Once the photos are finished, Santa goes into the unit where the *very* little ones are in the controlled environment of an incubator. These infants cannot even be removed from the unit. For these shots, Santa gets down to the child's level on the far side of the unit, while the photographer shoots through the plastic to record Santa's visit. The miracle children seem to get smaller every year. The tiniest child I have ever seen was less than 500 grams and born sixteen weeks premature.

The staff in the unit are wonderful. Little Santa hats, tiny Santa pyjamas and red-and-green blankets all come out when we record the child's first visit with Santa. The whole event takes several hours, and it is so important for everyone. Sadly, not all the children pull through this stage. In those instances, the photos will form a lifelong memory for parents and friends.

On the same floor of the hospital is the Pediatric Intensive Care Unit, where there might be children of any age. In 2012, when we had completed the NICU visit, a nurse asked me a simple question.

"Will you visit PICU, Santa? There is only one child." My answer was immediate.

"Of course!" Santa will visit wherever he is needed. The numbers of children, their names and even their conditions are not an issue. For each one, the visit is special – as we sense in this story from a mother of one of those children.

It was December 3ʳᵈ, sometime in the morning, when I heard that Santa was going to be visiting the babies in the NICU (the nursery) that day. Our son Jacob was in the PICU (intensive care) and he was the only patient. I had asked several nurses if Santa was going to be coming here today as well, and they didn't know – but they would certainly try to find one of Santa's helpers to find out.

Jacob was having a fussy day. The only place he wanted to be was up in Mommy's or Daddy's arms being rocked. If he was put in his crib at all he would cry, so we would pick him up again. Brian (his daddy) had decided to run home to get a quick bite to eat and shower, because we were spending every waking minute in the hospital, taking turns leaving for a few hours.

I remember Nurse Emily dressed in her shamrock scrubs at Christmas time coming in all excited from the hallway saying, "He's here and he's coming to visit Jacob." I was so excited that I immediately began to tear up. Our beautiful little boy was going to see Santa and have his picture taken. Two more nurses came over and said, "It's only for a short time, so we are going to take Jacob's oxygen off for the pictures."

Then, from just down the hallway, I heard Santa's bells and as they got closer I began to cry harder, just from pure excitement. Then he came through the door with his helpers right behind. Two nurses came over and took Jacob and placed him in Santa's arms. His helpers started taking some pictures, while I stood back and was so emotional that the nurses were coming over to comfort me.

Then I watched Jacob look up and stare at amazement at this white bearded man holding him, as if to say, "Wow! This is nice." Jacob was content. Then Santa started talking to him. At that moment I felt that

Jacob understood every word. Santa said he had a very special bear that he gives a special baby, and he would like to give it to Jacob.

Well, if Mommy had started to calm down, that went out the window. Now I started sobbing uncontrollably. At this point, the nurses took Jacob and put his oxygen back on. Then Santa came over and put his arms around me and said that Santa gives the best hugs – and boy, does he ever! It was an amazing experience, one I will never forget.

Five days later, on Saturday, December 8th, Jacob's three-month birthday, he was released from the hospital. Just as we were getting ready to leave, Santa's helper came in with the pictures they had taken a few days before.

On December 12th, just a few short days later, at home in his Mommy's and Daddy's arms, Jacob passed away due to being born with Edwards syndrome.

We are so grateful to have had Jacob's picture taken with Santa, and to have a special teddy bear to treasure forever – along with the wonderful memories Jacob gave us in the short three months and four days he was here with us.

So, thank you, Santa, for visiting our son Jacob and for giving us the memory that our little boy saw Santa before he passed away. Your teddy, the photos and our memories will be with us forever.

Valerie

Remembering Jason

No child in *The Man in the Red Suit* has been asked about as often as Jason. He is the little boy who sat crying outside Santa's change room, pleading for the door to be opened. I can still hear a loud female voice yelling and cursing as she came down the hall of the building. At the time, I thought I heard Jason being slapped. But I didn't *see* this happen, so I'll never be sure.

All this time, I sat in the dark, because I didn't want Jason to know I was in the room. Because if I *did* open the door, he would have seen me in my regular clothes – without the beard and all the other parts of my Santa outfit. That might have broken his heart. And even if I was still in my outfit, I couldn't take this child away from what might be an abusive home. The saddest part was that Jason stuck a note under the door before being taken away.

"I love you Santa, don't forget me, Santa. Please come and get me at Christmas."

I still have Jason's little note. I think of him often, and I regularly ask the social agency that sponsors the yearly party how this young boy is doing. There are privacy rules, which I fully understand. And there are regulations and laws about how these situations can be handled. Still, I wish there had been a different outcome from my visit. I do know the situation is monitored. In fact, I have been interviewed by the appropriate agencies about what *might* have happened that day.

In 2013, Santa visited the same support group at Christmas, but I called in advance to make sure my little friend was going to be there. (I only know his first name for client privacy reasons.) I asked that he meet Santa at the door, so he could take Santa's hand while we walked into the meeting room to see all the other children. When I got to the door, there was Jason – but he was carrying a one-year-old child on his hip.

"Hi, Santa. My sister had a baby boy, and he wants to meet Santa." So Jason took my other hand and the three of us went into the room. Jason took the baby to his young mother before he quickly returned to my side. The volunteers tell me that Jason has figured this to be his "survival technique." If he is carrying the baby, he feels pretty safe. Meanwhile, I understand that his dad has been released from jail. Slowly, I believe things are improving for Jason.

He stuck to me like glue as the names were called, helping me with each of the Christmas packages. He was polite and very keen to do a good job. When we finished handing out the presents, I reached into the big green bag and found some gift certificates for a local burger restaurant.

"Here you go, Jason. Santa has a special gift for a special elf. Take your buddies out for lunch." He looked at the certificates in disbelief.

"Thank you, Santa! I think about this time with you all year and you never let me down."

Jason, I think of you all year, too.

SANTA CLAUS OATH:
I realize that I belong to a brotherhood and will be
supportive, honest and show fellowship to my peers.

Chapter 19
Building a float

I t was a chilly March morning when I turned the ignition on in my car and headed to a business meeting in the east end of St. John's. March is usually the month when I start to think about the Santa Claus Parade. I know that sounds early, but there is a *lot* of work to be done.

Years ago, arranging floats for the parade was a much simpler exercise. There were many more family-owned businesses. Some of the national firms also had regional decision-makers who we would see at a Rotary meeting or a St. John's Board of Trade function. In a simpler time, businesses also had carpentry shops and display departments and people with time and talent. If you asked nicely, they could build a float sponsored by the company for the Santa Claus Parade.

Business is now growing very quickly in certain sectors in Newfoundland and Labrador. Because the resource sector is changing in St. John's, there are many new firms and buildings. The oil industry has brought prosperity and with it has come some generous help for our service clubs and charities. We appreciate the support of all firms, be they local, regional or national. But the employee resources available to companies is different than it was years ago.

Although there is support for the parade in the community, the shape of that support is changing. Business is much more competitive, with margins much thinner. There are fewer employees. Even with a strong and vibrant business community, firms have tighter budgets. Taking valuable employees' time to physically construct a float in the weeks leading up to the parade is getting more and more problematic.

However, it isn't all gloom and doom. We just need a different way of thinking about how to construct them. Fortunately, some senior managers consistently support the parade. They tell me their firm can supply financial support if the parade organizers can purchase the building materials and have the floats constructed. What is needed, of course, is a reliable workforce to construct the floats and mount them on a few flatbed trailers. Okay, Santa, how do we make this work? Well, the key is in "lateral thinking." Thinking outside the box and being creative in your solutions.

Meanwhile, back in my car, I head down the snow-covered road, being careful to avoid the ice and the city snow blowers still filling very large dump trucks from the most recent deluge. (In March, it stops looking pretty, and even Santa gets tired of shovelling!) When I turn onto Forest Road, there on my right is a large enclosure with high walls, barbed-wire fencing along the top, and a large green door able to accommodate large trucks. Uniformed personnel are moving in and out of the building. Then I see the sign: "Her Majesty's Penitentiary." Aha! A reliable workforce and an opportunity to teach inmates new skills. That's outside-the-box thinking!

I continue along until I find the address for my business meeting. When it's finished, I return to my office and immediately pick up the phone. I'm trying to reach the Superintendent of Prisons. Sometimes the stars all line up and you reach the right person. I ask for a meeting to see if it might be possible for the inmates to construct two of the floats inside the institution. We'll need to have them ready for the parade in eight months time. Happily, the superintendent agrees. In fact, he thinks he can help me create the team with the exact skills we need.

Along the way, he requests the proper authorizations through the Department of Justice. He asks for – and receives – the support of the wardens and the unions. He also suggests that I call the John Howard Society to engage their support. They are particularly helpful in showing me how I can provide receipts to corporations that are willing to support the project.

Next, we find a talented and very gifted designer who is known locally as Mr. Christmas. Eric is used to working with large displays of Christmas material in public buildings. He sees our "ask" as a design challenge. We ask him to create the design and materials list for two floats that will reflect the theme "Christmas Around the World." We also need him to draw and write out the specifications so that all of the parts can be cut, painted and assembled in the carpentry shop by inmates of the penitentiary. They have limited skills, but lots of enthusiasm. We estimate that the materials and design will cost about $5,000 per float.

Now it was time to go out to the business community. I drew up a list of companies where I hoped Santa might find support. I specifically needed three companies to come up with enough funding for two of the floats. So, my first call was to the Stirling family at NTV. For many years they have been faithful supporters by televising the parade and showing it multiple times over the Christmas holidays. I told them about our project and I submitted a plan in writing to the company for possible funding. Within a week I got a call to say they would finance one of the floats.

Next, I made an interesting call to the wonderful Patten family here at the A. Harvey Group of Companies. This amazing organization has backed not only their local community, but the whole province for a very long time. One of their companies is Browning Harvey Ltd., which is the bottler for Pepsi in Newfoundland and Labrador. I called to make my case – probably one of the dozens this company would receive every day. (Their email must get overloaded and the postman must struggle to deliver the requests to this amazing firm that does so much for charities and community projects.) Happily the answer was positive. They would definitely provide funds. Two companies down, one to go.

Bell Aliant is a terrific firm that supports our charitable community. I knew they had a focus on projects similar to our parade. In fact, their predecessor was Newfoundland Telephone, whose wonderful retirees are connected with the parade and with the Aliant Pioneers. (It also helps that our entire communications system for the parade is provided by Bell Aliant.) The parade organizers met with the staff at Her Majesty's Penitentiary, and in concert with the wonderful folks at John Howard they confirmed how a project like this involving the inmates would be good for the whole community. It would help the inmates build their skills, pride and their sense of self-worth. After our presentation to the executives at Bell Aliant, they gave us their full support. Now we had the resources to start the project.

Within the penitentiary staff, we especially needed support from the supervisor of the carpentry shop. First, the classification officers and the unit managers considered the skills that might be needed. Procedures had to be followed. The inmates were working with power tools and they were being trusted. However, the rule is: "We will treat you like men, if you act like men." As a result, there were some interesting perks. While the inmates were working on the project, radios played in the background. In the carpentry shop, there was a coffee machine, which the inmates were free to use.

Creating memories for children in the parade involves thousands of volunteers, with a wide range of skills and talents. Thanks to their hard work, more than 60,000 people saw two beautiful new floats in the parade. They won awards as two of the best in the entire parade. And here's one other special memory for me. One inmate realized his release date was actually going to arrive prior to the parade – so he volunteered to come back inside to finish the project. St. Nicholas would have been proud of him.

Chapter 20
Parlez-vous français, le Père Noël?

It was a predictably cold night in late December when Santa's sleigh pulled into the driveway at Ronald McDonald House in St. John's, Newfoundland. This is a familiar address. Santa and the wonderful people from the McDonald's Restaurants Canada® have been friends for a long time.

The story of these houses goes back to the city of Philadelphia in 1974. Fred and Fran Hill camped out on hospital benches and sat in cramped waiting rooms while their three-year-old daughter, Kim, went through three years of treatment for leukemia. The Hills watched other parents and families of seriously ill children do exactly the same thing. Many of the families had to travel long distances for their children to receive medical treatment. After all those expenses, they simply couldn't afford hotel rooms. The Hills knew there had to be a solution, so Fred rallied support to raise funds to buy an old house located near the hospital. It opened in 1974 as the first Ronald McDonald House. The network of these houses quickly grew.

In 2008, a feasibility study in Newfoundland and Labrador concluded that more than 115,000 patients had received health-care services at the Janeway in 2007. Twenty per cent of those patients had travelled more than 80 kilometres to receive care. Clearly there was an urgent need for a Ronald McDonald House in St. John's. Armed with this knowledge, a very determined group of people worked together. In September of 2012 there was a grand opening for Ronald McDonald House, Newfoundland and Labrador. This was Canada's fourteenth Ronald McDonald House. Now, Santa was thrilled to jump out of his sleigh to meet the wonderful staff for the second year in a row.

Santa waved to a full-size and lifelike Ronald McDonald figure sitting on a snow-covered bench in the driveway welcoming visitors. Then I opened the big friendly doors with the customary "Ho, Ho, Ho" greeting and the ringing of the bells. I timidly peeked around the living room door at the children's level to see who was there. This may seem like a strange thing to say, but there are only two visits a year when Santa hopes to see as few children as possible. One is Christmas Eve at the hospital itself, and the second is this party at Ronald McDonald House. There is only one place any child wants to be on Christmas Eve: home in their own bed. At the hospital and at Ronald McDonald House, all of the professionals work hard to make this happen.

On this 2013 visit, there were two little girls with their parents, along with the staff of the house.

"Regardez Lucille, il est le Père Noël," said the mother.

"Ah," said Santa. "Bonjour!" Then a staff member came forward to tell Santa that the house had a young visitor from St. Pierre and Miquelon. She did not speak any English. Well, this would be a new challenge!

Santa got down on the floor and encouraged his two young friends to join him. They were a little hesitant in the beginning, but Santa reached into his mailbag and he took out his worn but familiar copy of *'Twas The Night Before Christmas*. It's a pop-up book, so the pages leap to life as they are opened.

Then a woman approached Santa to offer some help.

"You just read, Santa," she coached. And I did.

"'Twas the night before Christmas and all through Ronald McDonald House," I began. Then, like magic, I heard another voice.

"C'était la nuit avant Noël et tout au long de Ronald McDonald House."

It was fascinating to see what happened next. With Santa lying on the floor, he encouraged the girls to do the same. One little girl stretched out on Santa's right side and the other on his left. There was giggling and laughing as we read this classic in both languages. Finally, we reached the end of the story.

"And I heard him exclaim as he drove out of sight, Merry Christmas to all and to all a good night." Then my elf assistant chimed in.

"Et je l'ai entendu hurler pendant qu'il conduisait hors de la vue, Joyeux Noël à tous et à tous une bonne nuit."

Then I asked the girls if they would like a ride on Santa's back. "Voulez-vous un tour sur le dos de Père Noël?"

The girls leapt up and jumped on Santa's back. The mothers laughed, the staff all laughed, and cameras clicked and recorded the fun. When it was time for Santa to go, the girls responded to Santa's request that they help the old man get up off the floor.

"Pouvez-vous aider le Père Noël sur le plancher?"

Santa waved goodbye and walked back out into the cold night. There sat Ronald McDonald in his friendly greeting pose. So I stopped for a moment.

"Joyeux Noël Ronald McDonald. Merci pour tout ce que vous faites pour les enfants du monde."

Chapter 21
Santa, will you hold Charlotte?

Hi Mr. Templeton,

It was nice to meet you on Saturday for your book signing! We brought our daughter Charlotte along to meet you. Santa had visited her in the Janeway Children's Health and Rehabilitation Centre in December 2002. It was her first Christmas. She was a preemie born in October that year and weighed just 542 grams.

I don't think I got the chance to say thank you for writing such a lovely book. I've only read a few pages so far. I have to wait until I get some time by myself as I'm sure I will need a box of tissues.

I happened to be on Google News one day when a headline about a man in a red suit caught my eye under local NL news. I clicked on it for curiosity, and as soon as I started reading the column it was like I was struck with a ton of bricks! I immediately began to cry as I knew what was coming next. So many emotions came flooding back about that time when Charlotte was at the Janeway. As we had mentioned on Saturday, there were many ups and downs during her stay there, but by the time December came she had vastly improved. Things were looking up!

You asked us on Saturday what it was like for us when Santa came to visit on Christmas Eve, and I wasn't able to put into words then and there exactly how we felt. But I remember hearing that Santa was coming to visit, and my husband John and I were like little kids ourselves. We were so excited! No parent ever expects their child's first Christmas to be spent at the Janeway, but when Santa came it was so uplifting. John and I just looked at each other, smiling and in awe. I remember as if it were yesterday.

We went home that night and we had such mixed emotions: sadness that we had to leave our baby on Christmas Eve, but also overjoyed and thankful she was doing so well and that there were people, such as you and the nurses and doctors, giving their time to visit and take care of her. Charlotte had her own little Christmas tree at the hospital, and we now have a family tradition. Every year we talk about her first Christmas and how Santa came to visit. Then she decorates her little tree, and we put it in a special place in our house to remind us of the miracle we received. She truly is a miracle. Every day she reminds us of how blessed we are to have her in our lives.

Christmas is such a special time for us. Not just for our little family of three but our extended family as well. Every year we gather with grandparents, aunts, uncles, cousins and good friends to celebrate and create new memories. It's not about the presents, the great food or the fancy decorations. It's about spending time with those we love, sharing traditions, and simply enjoying each other.

We were overjoyed when Charlotte was released from hospital after spending the first four months of her life there. It was a cold day in February when we took her home to our house in Torbay. We had lots of family and friends waiting there to welcome us home. It was a wonderful celebration. But after the celebration was over and everyone had gone home, we spent our first night alone with our daughter. It was eerily quiet. No alarms beeping, no quiet chatter of the nurses, no crying babies. We sort of looked at each other and said "Okay, what do we do now?" It's like the umbilical cord being cut all over again; leaving the warmth and protection of the Janeway and going out into the world. Who knew what lay ahead of us?

We quickly found our way, and as we settled into our routine of life we often found ourselves back on the steps of the Janeway. In fact, many times. Whether it was a trip to the emergency room or a regularly scheduled appointment, in some ways it felt like going back to see family. We would often take Charlotte to visit the NICU and show the doctors and nurses the fruits of their labour!

We still keep in touch with some of them. Often we've met an NICU nurse at the grocery store or somewhere else around town. They may not remember my name, but they say "You're Charlotte's mom, how's she doing?" They've seen many babies pass through their doors

and memories fade over time but one thing is for sure: We will NEVER forget our time there and everything that has been done for us. Even the little things like bringing us an ice cream treat while we sat by Charlotte's crib or having a visit from The Man in the Red Suit are memories we'll treasure forever.

I've attached a few extra pictures of Charlotte during her time at the Janeway and a couple from our visit with you on Saturday. There's one of her when she was just a few weeks old. You can see how tiny she is when her hand is touching my finger. Also, a photo of Charlotte in her Christmas stocking that she now hangs each year on the mantle eagerly awaiting Santa's arrival!

Thank you again for giving us this wonderful gift of your stories. Now I know for sure there really and truly is a Santa – not that there was ever any doubt!

All the best,

Andrea

SANTA CLAUS OATH:
I understand that the true and only gift
I can give, as Santa, is myself.

Chapter 22
Will you get out Santa?

anta's visits are generally timed to be an hour apart. The theory is that each visit will take about forty-five minutes, and the next one is usually about fifteen minutes away. The booking schedule starts in about March. By mid-October, the Saturdays and Sundays are pretty full. Then the whole adventure kicks off with the Santa Claus Parade on the last Sunday in November.

One year, I got a call from a lady in early September asking if Santa could go to a large apartment complex in St. John's. I got the impression that everything was being organized by volunteers. When Santa goes to a large corporate party, an executive assistant usually provides cell numbers, bottled water, a change room with a mirror and any number of items to make Santa's visit easier. Clearly, things were going to be different at the big apartment building – but that can just add to the fun.

My contact at the event set the date and time for Santa's visit, which I then logged into my computer. It was agreed that at exactly 2 p.m., Santa would knock loudly, pull open the big metal door, and shout "Merry Christmas!" Then, in mid-November, I got an email from a different person who was working at the same event. There was a big problem: the party room had been booked by two groups. They had to move their party up an hour, so could Santa now come at 1 p.m.?

Well, it isn't quite that simple. However, I figured if I could rearrange a prior visit, and shave a few minutes from that event, I could probably get to the apartment by 1:30 p.m. When I didn't hear anything further, I assumed this new schedule was okay. So I loaded the information from my computer into my BlackBerry and continued to take bookings for other events.

For a corporate visit, I usually get a series of confirmations and cell numbers of the organizers – just in case I am late or there is a problem. All I had from the apartment building was a November email and a contact name, but I had visited the group for the three previous years. So I assumed everything was fine. "Assume" is an awful word, as I was about to find out.

At 1:29 p.m. on the appointed day, I screeched into the apartment parking lot and rolled out of the sleigh. I went up to the big metal door, waited for the second hand to hit the twelve on my watch, and I pounded on the door. Then with great gusto, I pulled it open, rang my bells loudly, and shouted "Merry Christmas!"

Well, there's a first time for everything. I heard a loud shriek and then a woman shouting in a high-pitched voice.

"Sweet Jesus, there's two of you! Get out, Santa! Get out!"

She rushed over, spun me around, and pushed me back out through the door. As I flew over the doorframe, I heard a little girl in the background.

"Look, Mummy. Santa has a twin brother and they are both here!"

All I can say is, thank goodness for children and their wonderful imaginations!

Chapter 23
Christmas Eve in the Janeway Children's
Health and Rehabilitation Centre

O ver the last thirty-six years, Santa has probably made more than 1,500 visits to hospitals to visit with children. But all of those memories are recounted from Santa's perspective. I thought it was time to ask a nurse in the NICU to tell us her story. So I found someone special. Over the course of forty years, Sylvia has seen it all. Here are her recollections of Christmas Eve with these tiny infants.

Working Christmas Eve and being away from family can be difficult, but it is part of a nurse's life. It is not such a hardship, because we know that Santa is going to visit us. Our families know it, our children know it and our friends know it. And when it comes to Santa, we are all kids again for awhile. Christmas Eve at the Janeway NICU is the best night of the year. We see the true meaning of Christmas in our own unit. On that night someone who doesn't have to be there (but does anyway, for totally unselfish reasons) comes ringing down the hall. He simply cares about children.

It is just as exciting for the nurses in NICU to see Santa as it is for the parents. Last Christmas Eve, as soon as I heard the bells, I ran to the other room and said "Santa's here. Santa's here!" I already had my babies dressed in their Christmas outfits, and when I put babies in Santa's arms and see how he looks at them and holds their little thin hands, it touches my heart. He enjoys rocking the babies in the rocking chair and singing and smiling for the pictures taken by his doctor-daughter Christina and by the nurses, too. When babies are too sick to be put in Santa's arms, he stands behind the isolette, sometimes with the parents, for a picture.

Santa always takes time for any of the nurses who want pictures with him. He even calls their kids and grandkids at home and talks to them. We get such a wonderful feeling of the spirit of Christmas during Santa's visit that it lasts all through the night. It is a genuine privilege to be part of this very special evening, when our very own Santa comes to NICU.

Parents of a premature baby in NICU are stressed at the best of times, anxious and sometimes a little afraid of this tiny person who now consumes their energy every waking moment. Believe me, they don't get much sleep while their precious child is in hospital. They are often in awe and somewhat overwhelmed on Christmas Eve when Santa visits. They know he'll be there because we have been telling them for weeks. However, seeing is believing. And being invited to be in the picture with Santa and their baby just tops off the whole experience. This is a night that no parent will forget – when someone they don't know *is giving his Christmas to their child and giving them a most precious and everlasting memory.*

And what about these tiny little persons in NICU? How do they feel about Santa? Well, the nurses will tell you there is a magic and wonder in the air for these babies who might have been crying at the top of their little lungs when Santa arrived. Suddenly they become the calmest of God's little creatures when placed in Santa's arms. And, just like Santa could rock them all night, they are contented to stay right there – sound asleep.

So what is it like to work Christmas Eve at the Janeway if you are fortunate enough to be on the night shift? It is the best shift of the year. Why? Because Santa always visits.

My favorite Christmas Eve was when Santa talked to my grandson on the phone. I think I was more excited than he was. My daughter told me Christmas morning that he dropped the phone, said "I got to go to bed," and ran for the bedroom.

As for me, it has been a genuine privilege to have been part of this very special night over all these years when our own Santa comes to NICU.

One year during one of these hospital visits, Santa stood up from the big rocking chair and looked at his watch. It was approaching 10 p.m., but Santa still had a long night ahead. Suddenly the doors opened and two nurses in their green scrubs came in with a tiny child.

"Don't go, Santa. Little Andrew was born fifteen minutes ago. The rest of the family is on the way to see their new little brother. His parents want his picture taken with Santa!"

Santa sat down for this special moment. It was Christmas Eve and this child was born on a moonlit night. How amazing!

Then Santa went to an office in the building where there was a big suitcase. A few minutes later, my doctor-daughter and I wheeled out of the hospital. It was a ten-minute drive to our church, but we arrived at 10:58 p.m. – with two minutes to spare. I looked at the stained glass windows. I listened as the organist played his Christmas prelude. Then we all sang "Silent Night, Holy Night."

I knew that other than sending Santa off to the dry-cleaner, another wonderful year was complete.

Acknowledgements

There are people and organizations who work tirelessly with me to make and deliver Santa's seasonal adventures.

The first is my wife Paula who stoically endures my Santa pursuits almost daily all year! She has the patience of a saint! She puts up with a lot and has a hawk eye for spelling, grammatical and punctuation mistakes. Yes, she has read this book!

My daughter Dr. Christina Templeton is at Santa's side through every door in the Janeway Children's Health and Rehabilitation Centre on Christmas Eve. While observing the strict code of privacy demanded in her profession, she only needs to gently nod and Santa knows that a teddy bear should stay with a particular child. Sometimes, an obituary appears a few days later.

I should acknowledge the support of Rotary International (RI) and the Rotary Clubs in Newfoundland and Labrador. RI is fully committed to the eradication of polio in the world and we are "this close." However, when I took the money from the initial printing of the first book and told local clubs that a contribution was to be made to Rotary International's Polio Plus Campaign, the clubs matched my contribution and a considerably larger contribution went forward.

I acknowledge my publisher Creative Book Publishing and the team led by Donna Francis. Pam Dooley does all things marketing and what you hold in your hand has the artistry of Todd

Manning and Joanne Snook-Hann. My social media advisor Josh Jamieson does all the magic with Facebook and Twitter.

For the second time, I placed my manuscript in the hands of gifted editors and they have turned a lump of coal into something very special. Thank you both. You are wordsmiths and I truly appreciate everything you have done.

I wish to especially thank Sister Elizabeth Davis for not only writing the foreword but for her support for many years. She understands what I am trying to do as she sees it through the many phases of her own experience. Sister Elizabeth Davis RSM is the Congregational Leader Sisters of Mercy Generalate and has traveled the world for her congregation. From 1994 to 2000 she was the President and CEO of the Health Corporation of St. John's, so she understands of the work of St. Nicholas from many different angles.

Thank you also to Cathy Bennett, MHA; to Toni Marie Wiseman and to Shannie Duff for reading the manuscript and for encouraging the publishing of the work.

There is the team that puts the Santa Claus Parade together. That too starts in late spring with the Downtown Development Commission and the efficient staff of Gaylynne Lambert and Scott Cluney. Yes, two people coach and lead a massive number of volunteers to get ready for Santa's arrival.

For many years, Santa has counted on the pilots and ground crew of Universal Helicopter Newfoundland Limited. When a child looks up above the parade and a figure is waving in a red suit and hanging out the door of a real helicopter, then the real Santa must be here.

Along the parade route and at the beginning of the parade, amazing volunteers from Newfoundland Power push the supermarket carts and pick up the tons of food brought along by 60,000 people who generally show up for the parade. And the president of the company, Santa's Elf Earl, is there along with his wonderful team of Newfoundland Power employees to make sure this important part of the parade is a seamless success.

The Rovers Search and Rescue is a group of about fifty very well-trained personnel who are skilled at crowd control and communication. They plan the security, co-ordinate road closures, and work closely with the Royal Newfoundland Constabulary to make sure that no child gets lost or hurt in all the excitement of parade day.

Elf 342 is another faithful and tireless supporter of Santa's. This wonderful elf is a business owner and through some magic means each year she delivers thirty-six beautiful teddy bears to Santa. Then beautiful red scarves are added from the team at Embroidme on Water Street. Most of the teddy bears are given away at the hospital or to a child to whom something serious has happened in their lives. When Santa goes to a school, the teachers know that Santa can bring a little something special to a needy child and without giving me any of the details or breaking the ever-tightening rules of privacy,

I am steered to a child in one particular classroom and a gentle nod indicates who the recipient should be. In most instances, there has been a recent family death or sudden separation of a loved one from the child.

Santa has a team that keep him flawless. Thank you to wonderful supporters Lahey's Hairstyling, Tony's Tailor Shop, Modern Shoe Hospital and Custom Dry Cleaners.

And finally, there is a critical team, a ministry team that assists St. Nicholas and Santa. The pastoral team at the hospitals and especially Rev. Dr. David Sutherland at St. Andrew's Presbyterian Church who helps when the journey gets to be unclear. I sometimes go back and read the letters from parents who have been there and it confirms that while this may be a small "m" ministry, it is an important one none the less.

Bibliography

Guinn, Jeff. *The Autobiography of Santa Claus.* New York: Penguin, 2005. Print.

Chris, Teresa. *The Story of Santa Claus.* London: New Burlington Books, 1992. Print.

English, C. Adam. *The Saint Who Would Be Santa Claus.* Waco: Baylor University Press. Print.

Nast, Thomas. *Thomas Nast's Christmas Drawings.* New York: Dover Publications. Print.

Photo and Trademark Credits

Trademark Acknowledgements

"Christmas in Heaven" used with permission of the author Wanda White (Bencke). Copyright 1997.

"The Hockey Song" Written by Tom C. Connors. Crown-Vetch Publishing (SOCAN). Licensed via StompinTom.com. Copyright 1971.

"Let There Be Peace on Earth" by Jill Jackson and Sy Miller. Copyright 1955, 1983 by Jan-Lee Music (ASCAP); International copyright secured. Used by Permission; all rights reserved.